Right You Are

Alfred Drake as Laudisi in the Westport production, 1952
directed by Eric Bentley

Right You Are

COSÍ È (SE VI PARE)

by LUIGI PIRANDELLO

A Stage Version with an Introduction and Notes
by ERIC BENTLEY

Associate Professor of English in Columbia University

COLUMBIA UNIVERSITY PRESS

New York 1954

≠ 780627

COLUMBIA BICENTENNIAL EDITIONS AND STUDIES

The Energetics of Development
BY LESTER G. BARTH AND LUCENA J. BARTH

New Letters of Berlioz, 1830–1868
TEXT WITH TRANSLATION, EDITED BY JACQUES BARZUN

On the Determination of Molecular Weights by Sedimentation and Diffusion
BY CHARLES O. BECKMANN AND OTHERS

LUIGI PIRANDELLO: *Right You Are*
TRANSLATED AND EDITED BY ERIC BENTLEY

The Sculpture of the Hellenistic Age
BY MARGARETE BIEBER

The Algebraic Theory of Spinors
BY CLAUDE C. CHEVALLEY

HENRY CARTER ADAMS: *Relation of the State to Industrial Action* AND *Economics and Jurisprudence*
EDITED BY JOSEPH DORFMAN

ERNST CASSIRER: *The Question of Jean-Jacques Rousseau*
TRANSLATED AND EDITED BY PETER GAY

The Language of Taxonomy
BY JOHN R. GREGG

Ancilla to Classical Reading
BY MOSES HADAS

JAMES JOYCE: *Chamber Music*
EDITED BY WILLIAM Y. TINDALL

Apocrimata: Decisions of Septimius Severus on Legal Matters
EDITED BY WILLIAM L. WESTERMANN AND A. ARTHUR SCHILLER

General Editor's Preface

THE modern university has become a great engine of public service. Its faculty of Science is expected to work for our health, comfort, and defense. Its faculty of Arts is supposed to delight us with plays and exhibits and to provide us with critical opinions, if not to lead in community singing. And its faculty of Political Science is called on to advise government and laity on the pressing problems of the hour. It is unquestionably right that the twentieth-century university should play this practical role.

But this conspicuous discharge of social duties has the effect of obscuring from the public—and sometimes from itself—the university's primary task, the fundamental work upon which all the other services depend. That primary task, that fundamental work, is Scholarship. In the laboratory this is called pure science; in the study and the classroom, it is research and teaching. For teaching no less than research demands original thought, and addressing students is equally a form of publication. Whatever the form or the medium, the university's power to serve the public presupposes the continuity of scholarship; and this in turn implies its encouragement. By its policy, a university may favor or hinder the birth of new truth. This is the whole meaning of the age-old struggle for academic freedom, not to mention the age-old myth of academic retreat from the noisy world.

Since these conditions of freedom constitute the main theme of Columbia University's Bicentennial celebration, and since the university has long been engaged in enterprises of public moment, it was doubly fitting that recognition be given to the activity that enlarges the world's "access to knowledge." Accordingly, the Trustees of the University and the Directors of its Press decided to signalize the 200th year of Columbia's existence by publishing some samples of current scholarship. A full representation was impossible: limitations of time and space exercised an arbitrary choice. Yet the Bicentennial Editions and Studies, of which the titles are listed on a neighboring page, disclose the variety of products that come into being on the campus of a large university within a chosen year. From papyrology to the determination of molecular weights, and from the state's industrial relations to the study of an artist's or poet's work in its progress toward perfection, scholarship exemplifies the meaning of free activity, and seeks no other justification than the value of its fruits.

JACQUES BARZUN

Introduction

ON the face of it, *Right You Are* is the purest instance of "drama of ideas" in the history of the theatre, a veritable exhibition of an idea, the statement of a proposition—namely, that truth is relative and subjective: what seems to me, or you, to be so *is* so. The statement is made in the (Italian) title, explained by a leading character (Laudisi), and embodied in what the author himself designates a parable. Pirandello seems as single-minded as Aesop, his parable a simple fable, apologue, or exemplum.

If it is rare to find a play so deliberately dedicated to a principle, it is rarer to find one dedicated to a principle that none of us will assent to. What would "assent" mean, anyway? That a certain principle which "seems so" to Pirandello also "seems so" to you or me? What if it did? How can we be sure that it is the same principle as the one he is talking about? Furthermore, if *Right You Are* is true only for Pirandello, why did he write it down? If a man holds the view that views are incommunicable, how can he hope to communicate *that* view? In short, we could not assent to the idea of *Right You Are* even if we would.

Was Pirandello a fool? Had he not taken that elementary lesson in philosophy in which the instructor triumphs over relativism and scepticism by observing that relativism must not become absolute and that the sceptic should be sceptical of scepticism? There is evidence on the point—for example, the following debate:

A: The world is my idea (*rappresentazione*), and the world is purely ideal (*una idealità*) . . . The world—all

that is external to the ego—exists only according to the idea
one has of it. I do not see what is; what I see, is.

B: Or is not, my dear fellow. Because you may see badly.
That existences outside ours should be little more than ap-
pearances without reality outside the ego is supposed by the
champions of an idealism which the English call solipsism,
and you know that it isn't a new notion—English writers following the philosophy of Berkeley have given it fantastic
form. And you will know *Through the Looking Glass.* Suppose, my dear fellow, that I, let us say, do not exist outside
your ego except as you see me? This means that your consciousness is one-sided, that you are not conscious of me,
that you have no *realization* of me within you (to use an expression of Josiah Royce), that your idea does not live for
me.

And it must be so. And here, to turn to art, is our true point
of difference. For me the world is not solely ideal, that is,
it is not confined to the notion I can form of it: outside me
the world exists of itself and alongside me; and in my
representation or idea of the world I am to propose to *realize*
it as much as I can, creating for myself a consciousness in
which it exists—in me as in itself, seeing it as it sees itself,
feeling it as it feels itself. And so, nothing symbolic and ap-
parent for me, everything will be real and alive!

Since Pirandello * is not *A* but *B* we are forced, I
think, to admit that he knew what he was doing and are
free to ask: if the relativism is a joke, what is serious
in the play? In the midst of an earnest discussion in a
Westport home, someone appealed to the maid who
was bringing in the tea things, "What did *you* get out
of *Right You Are?*" "I guess it just says, keep your
nose out of other folks' business," she replied, thus
proving all over again how right Molière was to con-
sult his cook. Such is indeed the simple message not
only implicit in the action of the play but explicitly

* Writing in the weekly journal *Il Marzocco*, March 7, 1897, in reply
to Ugo Ojetti *(A)*, *Il Marzocco*, February 28, 1897.

stated by Laudisi at the outset as the serious moral conclusion to the frivolous philosophical argument. "Respect what other people see and touch even if it's the
opposite of what you see and touch" (p. 19). The
reader should go on to ask, as the actor must, not only
what Laudisi says but what he does. For more than two
acts, he tries to discourage people from interfering
with the lives of others. In the third act, he decides that
talk is useless, but his goal is unchanged: he hopes that
a coup de théâtre may succeed where reason failed—
succeed in demonstrating the wickedness and futility
of interference.

Pirandello once said he wanted the play to indicate
the triumph of the imagination over mere facts. But the
imagination he shows us is not a philosophical or lit-
erary power of imagining what is not, it is insight into
what is, insight by means of sympathy, it is compassion, it is love. While the ostensible principle of his
play is an unacceptable metaphysic, the real principle
is: love your neighbor. To realize how far truth is subjective is to realize that one must respect the subject.
Pirandello is defending the person against the dehu-
manizing influence of society. His special care is for
the sanctity of the intimate affections, the right to pos-
sess your soul in peace and privacy. These ideas are
as old as *Antigone* but have become more relevant than
ever with the rise of the police state. And it is not just
fanatics—Communists or the persecutors of Communists—who are open to attack. "Many of our best
friends" have for years been boosting the public interest and the objective fact above the private interest and
the subjective fact. The inner life of man has been
neglected and mocked, without any perceptible public
gain.

The seemingly cryptic figure of the veiled lady in *Right You Are* is perhaps the simplest expression of indignation at this neglect in modern literature. She is the inner sanctum, the holy of holies. Her life being love, she has achieved complete self-sacrifice, she has no identity; she exists only in relationship, she is wife to the husband, daughter to the mother; she is what the husband thinks she is, she is what the mother thinks she is, she is what *you* think she is. On the literal plane, all this is absurd, of course, yet hardly more so than the rest of the play. It is all—to quote Pirandello's own perfect characterization—*una gran diavoleria*, a big joke, a piece of deviltry.

Now under what circumstances does a man champion a philosophy he knows to be fallacious? When he wants to enjoy himself and throw ideas about like colored balls. "You're simply being paradoxical," we say to a friend who champions an error with gusto. But the truth is *not* simple. Part of it is that he has been enjoying the comedy of intellect. Another part is that by stating an error he wants to make you more aware of the truth. Laudisi is not quite a devil's advocate. His method is more like the inverse of a reductio ad absurdum: he doesn't take plausible premises and prove that they lead to disastrous consequences, he takes implausible premises and derives very desirable consequences from them. We have seen how he derives from his "absolute relativism" the principle of the golden rule. It is also important to see the totality of Laudisi's speeches in the context of other characters' speeches. Laudisi constitutes a sort of frame for the picture or—more correctly perhaps—the spectacles we see the picture through.

Once the "deviltry" of the play is conceded, even its

final leap into the realm of symbol seems fully justi-
fied. The audience may be cheated of the answer it is
waiting for, but it accepts the *image* of the veiled lady
unquestioningly. At that point, in performance, there
is usually a gasp of astonishment signaling to the actors that the bullet has shot home. And nothing could
better illustrate what this play is like than the fact that
its climax is an image. If our first discovery is that the
idea of the play is not "truth is relative" but "love your
neighbor," our second is that *Right You Are* is not, in
any narrow sense, a "drama of ideas" at all. To convince himself he had ideas, Pirandello had to redefine
the term. "An artist's 'ideas,' " he wrote in his essay
on humor, "are not abstract ideas but feelings, senti-
ments, which become the center of his inner life, take
hold of his spirit, shake it, and, by shaking it, create
a body of images." *Six Characters in Search of an Author* seems to have started in Pirandello's mind with an
image of Madama Pace's establishment which he took
a note of in 1910. He also tells us that *Right You Are*
was born from "the frightening image" in a dream of
"a deep courtyard with no exit." * It is with the imagination, not the ratiocinative faculty, that this courtyard
is transformed into the home of the Ponzas (the idea of
"no exit" being left to Jean Paul Sartre).

For Pirandello was an artist and, in the fullest pro-
fessional sense, a playwright. He described one of his
plays as "Pinero with a difference," and *Right You
Are* is a thriller, almost a who-done-it—with a difference. The audience modestly identifies itself with the
foolish busybodies, anxiously asks: Is the girl *her*
daughter or *his* second wife?—is led to the one answer
and the other in rapid alternation, only to be authori-

* See *Almanacco Letterario Bompiani*, 1938.

tatively told at the end that the girl is *both* her daughter
and his second wife. Luckily, there is another "difference" besides the famous ending—that this thriller
contains two other dramas, a tragedy and a comedy.

The tragic action of *Right You Are,* bounded by the
arrival and departure of the Ponza-Frola family, derives from an unknown "misfortune"; the exposure of
three lives to the public gaze re-opens the wound; they
decide to leave.

The comic action derives from the conflict between
Laudisi and the townspeople (principally, of course,
his own family). The three acts correspond to three
stages in this conflict. In the first, the "crowd"—in effect a chorus—investigates the lives of the unhappy trio
to the point where two of them come forward in turn
and make confessions. In the second, the crowd has the
"great idea" of confronting Ponza and Frola. Up to
this point, Laudisi has practiced dissuasion. But when,
in the third act, the police commissioner refuses to
write a fictitious explanation that will satisfy everyone's curiosity, Laudisi the peacemaker becomes Laudisi the mischief-maker. He caps the coups de théâtre
of the first two acts with an even greater one by giving
Sirelli the idea of bringing over Signora Ponza. At the
end, his point is proved and he is victor.

This comic action is repetitious. Yet, if Acts One
and Two of Pirandello's play present the same drama
three times, the very fact that unfriendly critics are
not bored but irritated suggests a positive process
rather than merely the author's inability to think of
something else to say. For one thing, it is repetition
and *change*—change in speed and change in magni-
tude. Farce (and this is farce-comedy) is a mecha-

nism very like many of the weird and whirling vehicles of a fairground. Its favorite trick is acceleration to a climax—which is reached, in Pirandello's play, just before the final meeting of the Ponzas and Signora Frola. In each act, the same drama takes place: the Ponza-Frolas are the actors, the townspeople the audience. But it is a bigger, "louder" drama every time. And the tempo is stepped up. Now, while the repetition that stems from sterility merely bores, positive repetition, especially when accompanied by a crescendo and an accelerando, is dangerously full of life and tends to act directly on the nervous system. In more Dionysian works—say in O'Neill's *Emperor Jones* or Ravel's *Bolero*—this is readily admitted. What we are less ready to see is the manic element in *comic* repetition. Perhaps the final subtlety of *Right You Are* is that the sad and sinister traits that are overt in the Ponza-Frola story lurk also in the farce that frames it; hysteria and madness are not far below the surface. However this may be, manic repetition is of the essence of farce—as any page of Molière's prose will testify. John Gay's Macheath is arrested, not once, but twice, the second arrest being superfluous by the standards of modern dramaturgy, but integral to the pattern of classic farce-comedy. A farce-comedy consists of concentric circles of repetition: around the inner ring of phrases, the outer ring of incidents.

In taking Laudisi to be a comic character, I do not mean that he should be continuously funny but that such a figure is closer to the tradition of clowning than to that of wise uncles, doctor friends, and ministering psychoanalysts. Tell the actor of this part that Laudisi is a *raisonneur,* and you will get spectacles, an avuncu-

lar manner, prosy explanatoriness; the philosophy will
ride him, not he it. Laudisi is Harlequin * in modern
dress, a Harlequin who has invaded the realm of philosophy, and who behaves there as he had behaved
elsewhere. All his scenes are gags—from the little epi-
sode in which he teaches the Sirellis philosophy (pp.
14–20), through the mirror scene, the butler scene,
and the scene with Signora Cini and Signora Nenni on
the couch, all the way to his inventing of a ghost story
(pp. 103–104) and actual raising up of a ghost. He is
what the Italian theatre calls a *brillante,* and should
sparkle. He needs the bounding energy, the diabolical
rhythm, that we associate with the tradition of the commedia dell'arte. The challenge of the part today is that
it needs these things much more than what we usually
require of our serious actors: subtlety of characterization. The actor of the role of Laudisi does not have the
task of helping the audience to understand a complex
person with such and such a life history; he serves,
rather, the more technical function of a link between
the comic chorus and the tragic trio, and also between
the action onstage and the audience. He needs a highly
developed technique because he has to turn like light-
ning from one activity to another, from one interlocu-
tor to another, to effect transitions from triviality to
seriousness, from tears to laughter, and in the last act
to take the play and lift it into the world of fantasy. He
needs a personality of strength as well as charm because his presence has to be felt even when he is silent
and still.

From the two groups into which the rest of the cast

---

* Harlequin is the only name that conveys to the general reader the
notion of a character from the commedia dell'arte. Laudisi is actually
closer to the mischief-making Brighella, ancestor of Scapin and Figaro,
than to Arlecchino.

falls, the play demands two distinct ways of acting.
One group must play tragedy with a tempestuousness
forgotten on our Anglo-American stage and believed to
be somewhat foreign to our temperament. The part of
Ponza presents the Stanislavsky-trained actor with a
teasing problem: what to do about the motivation of
a character whose motivation is a mystery? I suppose
such an actor can invent motives out of whole cloth, but
a pre-Stanislavsky actor, for whom such questions did
not arise, would be in a simpler position; he need not
ask why Ponza is nearly fainting (page 85), he can
just take Pirandello's word for it. Pirandello is pointedly uninterested in the final psychological explanation of Ponza's passion, he is presenting the passion
itself. The actor's task is to do likewise—and to do it
within the imposed frame of a social type (the white-
collar worker). Fernand Ledoux at the Comédie Française has shown that it can be done. Yet, to be sure,
the alarming Latin way in which emotion leaps from
pianissimo to fortissimo in so few words presents the
non-Latin actor with a problem. In all modern drama
there is nothing harder to do—or even to decide *how*
to do—than the final meeting and exit of the tragic
trio.

No less forgotten and just as often considered foreign (usually French) is the style of comedy required
from the second group of actors. Here again it is futile
to hunt the motive. The actor's attention has to be transferred from individual psychology where nowadays it
too often concentrates itself on to the task of cooperation with other actors in a matter of craftsmanship. He
must suspend his belief that it is harder and better to act
a Chekhov role than that of a Keystone cop. He must not
resist Pirandello's method by complaining that the

characters are not sufficiently individualized. Who ever said the Keystone cops were not sufficiently individualized? One could praise them for not being *excessively* individualized; though any one of them could always step out of the group and have just as much individuality as he needed.

An author who insists on a character being six feet one and having an I.Q. of 120 may be said to be creating "closed" characters; an author who leaves the actor large leeway is creating open ones. Traditionally, the theatre deals in open characters; the author's points can be made in a dozen different ways—with actors of different physique using different "line-readings," and so forth. The members of Pirandello's chorus are open characters. Each actor can try his own way of making the main point (Agazzi's self-importance, for example), and it is for the director to decide if the attempt is in place. The nine actors concerned can be asked to make a quick study of their parts and come to rehearsal each with a creation—a Daumier portrait, as it were. In rehearsal it is discovered whether these creations work. If and when they begin to do so, they have to be coordinated. Comic characters most commonly run in pairs. Sirelli is a crony of Agazzi, Signora Cini of Signora Sirelli, Signora Nenni of Signora Cini: ideally all these pairs would become comic couples enjoying as easy and active a relationship as comedian and straight man in vaudeville. A part like that of Signora Sirelli, which barely catches the attention of the reader, in a production by a *maître* like Dullin, becomes a Dickensian gem. The richness of the part stems, technically speaking, from the fact that the actress can play three distinct relationships—to her husband (whom she bickers with), to Laudisi (whom she flirts with), to Cini (whom she patronizes).

No particular style should be imposed on the actors or even spoken of. A true style will come, if at all, as the bloom on a fruit that has ripened by natural growth and good gardening. You can no more tell an actor to perform with style than you can tell him to be funny. And stylization is the last refuge of the theatrical charlatan. Artificial speech and gesture that can be imposed by decree are not worth decreeing. Such "artificial" style as we have admired—say Gielgud in Wilde—is the product, not of a decree, but of practice.

The nine chorus members of *Right You Are* will bring with them (one hopes) a technique acquired in farce or vaudeville, but they will not at once be permitted to display their antics because this play needs (as what play does not?) a certain air of naturalness; only thus can the unnatural and macabre elements have their full effect. Hence the primary aim of the acting must be social satire: we are moving in middle-class circles in a provincial town.

Some caricaturists start with an exact likeness. When they later distort and exaggerate, they take their cue from the truth: only a long nose is made longer, only a small eye smaller, a fat man fatter. This principle applies to the chorus characters in *Right You Are* —and to the stage design.

I want my designer to give me an actual room belonging to the right time and place—not necessarily the room in every detail, but enough to suggest its solid, corporeal presence. He must not "stylize" the room with playful fancies of his own. (A common mistake of playful designers is to caricature the pictures on the wall. If the point is, for example, that a picture is sentimental, an actual picture, well chosen, would make the point more forcibly. Openly to make the picture ridiculous is to insult the spectator by instructing him how to respond. And of all instructions, "Now laugh!" is the most risky. The quantity of laughter out front is generally in inverse ratio to that on stage. "Chuckle-some" productions are sepulchral.) The stage design-er's legitimate distortion of actuality must take the form of omission of the unnecessary, and concentra-tion on the necessary, elements.

"What do the characters *do* onstage?" I was asked by a famous actor who was worried at the absence in the script of all allusion to eating, drinking, and smok-ing, and the various activities which his naturalistic technique would be helpless without. I do not believe the answer is to insert them; they contribute nothing. "Necessary" means "necessary to the play as Piran-dello conceived it," a classic comedy, an elemental tragedy, a slender thriller—anything but a piece of genre painting. What do these people do? They gossip. The furniture of gossip is—the chair. It therefore seemed to me in keeping with Pirandello's almost fa-natic leanmindedness to provide the actors with noth-ing but chairs. Lester Polakov * wished to fill the stage with monstrous chairs, their backs five or six feet high, so that the actors would spend the evening threading their way through a forest of furniture. The high backs would mask so much of the stage that the "blocking" problem would be enormous. But some day the idea should be tried.

In both my productions I raised the curtain on an unpeopled stage with a ring of chairs in the center fac-ing inwards to suggest that, the day before, perhaps, a circle of gossips had sat there with their heads together. During the first scene Amalia and Dina are rearrang-ing the chairs in a semicircle, and from here on, the

* Designer of many productions for Columbia Theater Associates, Columbia University.

chief physical action was the grouping and re-grouping of the chairs; for not only is the whole crowd always gossiping, but the Agazzi family is forever receiving visitors, forever setting the stage for the latest drama and preparing an "auditorium" for the onlookers. It seems apt to give Agazzi and his wife a nervous passion for re-ordering their room. In addition to satirizing the lower-middle-class love of tidiness and symmetry, it is an external, theatrical equivalent of the inner tension and fever.

In Act One, the interviews with Ponza and Frola are presented with the chorus forming a semicircle and the object of their scrutiny occupying the only remaining seat, the piano stool, in the middle. In my mind I had the image of an operating room with watching students. In Act Two Pirandello has written a scene with Laudisi on a couch between two ladies. I decided to make the couch the cynosure of all eyes throughout the act by having Agazzi choose it as the projected meeting place for Ponza and Frola. The actual meeting takes place in the open space in front, the chorus standing behind the couch and semicircle of chairs. Here I had in mind a prize ring with a crowd around—or animals in a cage before a crowd of onlookers. The third act is essentially that old standby among theatrical scenes—a trial scene. The drawing room becomes a sort of court of appeals with the Governor as the chief justice. Accordingly, I brought the one large table of the set out of its corner and placed it at right angles to the audience near stage center. When the Governor sat behind it, flanked by Centuri, Agazzi, and Sirelli, a bench of judges was readily suggested.

I shall not detain the reader with the minor details of my scheme. They were not the same in the two productions I did, nor would they be the same in any future production. The scheme itself is but one possibility among many. I should be interested in trying, sometime, a more naturalistic treatment. Given a cast of trained clowns, I should also be interested in trying a *less* naturalistic treatment: I can imagine a chorus of comedians jumping up and sitting down like jack-in-the-boxes. Directors understandably stress the tragedy more or the comedy more, according to the special abilities of the actors on hand. The French production I saw was delightful light comedy; my own productions seemed to succeed better on the tragic side. The ideal production that one should aim at would be no compromise or half-way house between tragedy and comedy, drama and farce, but a synthesis of the two. I even think I know how the synthesis might be arrived at, and that is by casting English character actors as the chorus, and American realistic actors as Ponza and Frola. (I would then keep the whole cast on to do *Six Characters* with the same dual distribution. And so I find myself making the conventional plea for cooperation between the English-speaking peoples.)

I have dwelt on the practicalities of staging because no playwright of our time has had a mind more utterly theatrical. In the Appendix I discuss the short story which *Right You Are* is based on and find the theatrical version better. An artist of course does not go from one medium to another out of a desire for something better but out of a need for something other. Almost until he wrote *Right You Are* Pirandello said he would not write plays; he feared those misinterpretations at the hands of actors which he later depicted in *Six Characters*. Even after *Right You Are,* he spoke of the plays as a "parenthesis" within the writing of his fiction. If in the latter part of his career he was more a playwright

than a story writer it was because the drama—much as
he resisted it—corresponded to his vision of life. A
poet, whose mind worked in images, he was obsessed,
or inspired, by one master-image: that of the theatre.
From it he ultimately elaborated his "trilogy of the
theatre in the theatre." But already in *Right You Are,*
when we see Ponza acting out his drama before his
drawing room audience, we are witnessing "theatre in
the theatre."

The notion that "all the world's a stage and all the
men and women merely players" is one of the com-
monplaces of western civilization. A charming version
of it in Italian runs:

> mondo è teatro e l'uomo è marionetta:
> se voi guardate bene nella vita
> ognun vi rappresenta una scenetta

At this late date a restatement of the commonplace
would itself be commonplace; Pirandello's vision finds
expression in a special application of it. To say that a
man is an actor is normally to condemn him, and the
normal procedure of criticism, satire, comedy, is to
remove his mask. Pirandello's play *Vestire gli ignudi,*
following Ibsen's *Wild Duck,* shows the calamitous
consequences of so doing. The collective title of his
plays is *Maschere nude (Naked Masks).* People mask
the fact that they are masked; Pirandello strips this
fact bare and excuses it. The "mask" of his title resem-
bles the *fantasma* (fantasy, ghost) of Laudisi, the *pupo*
(puppet) of Ciampa (who is the Laudisi of *Cap and
Bells*), the *pagliacetto* (doll) of Diego Cinci (who is
the Laudisi of *Each in His Own Way*). Laudisi's mirror speech makes it clear that error consists, not in
having a ghost, wearing a mask, but in chasing *il fantasma altrui,* the ghosts of other people, the masks of

others, in the belief that these are not ghosts and masks, but souls and faces. That there *is* a soul, a center of identity, is not questioned by Diego Cinci at least, for he denounces the false mask of one Prestino on the grounds that it does not correspond with what he "really is and can be."

The word *maschera* is also used to define the actors of the commedia dell'arte who each played one fixed role. The critic who said Pirandello was not interested in characters but in *maschere* (see p. 136) probably meant pretty much what people mean when they damn an author for creating "types," not "individuals": types are assumed to be characters of contemptible cardboard, mere snap judgments on social groups. The roles of the commedia are a great deal more. They offer as fair a field to the psychologist as any of the modern typologies, and like the latter they represent a delving below both individual and social distinctions for the very elements of our humanity. Now, several of Pirandello's critics (first among them Bontempelli, I believe) have noticed the elemental quality in his Ponzas and Frolas and have recorded their impression that the maestro has rendered human nature in its raw and general state prior to individuation. This being so, one is tempted to take the *maschere* in the phrase *maschere nude* to mean the human archetypes, human beings stripped of the accretions of civilization. If this isn't what Pirandello meant, it is, so to say, what he ought to have meant. He had every right to claim that he dealt in such archetypes—if only, by the nature of the case, gropingly, by intuition. And the chief function of the theatre in Pirandello's life was that it helped him to do so.   E.B.

Columbia University
Summer, 1953

Contents

Illustrations

Right You Are

Characters

THE GOVERNOR *of the Province*

CENTURI *Police Commissioner*

COUNCILLOR AGAZZI

DINA *his daughter*

AMALIA *his wife*

LAMBERTO LAUDISI *her brother*

SIGNOR PONZA *an executive secretary under* AGAZZI

SIGNORA PONZA *his wife*

SIGNORA FROLA *his mother-in-law*

SIGNOR SIRELLI
SIGNORA SIRELLI } *friends of the* AGAZZIS'

SIGNORA CINI *a friend of* SIGNORA SIRELLI'S

SIGNORA NENNI *a friend of* SIGNORA CINI'S

BUTLER

A MAN

A SECOND MAN

OTHER CITIZENS

THE PLACE: *A province in central Italy*

THE TIME: *The present*

Act I~Scene 1

The curtain rises on the home of Councillor Agazzi. In the drawing room are AMALIA, DINA, *and* LAUDISI. *Laudisi is walking across the room, irritated. A man of about forty, quick and lithe, he dresses well without overdoing it; he has on a violet-colored smoking jacket with black lapels and braid.*

LAUDISI

Aha! So he's gone to take the matter up with the Governor?

AMALIA

[*About forty-five, grey hair. Makes a great show of importance because of her husband's place in society, at the same time giving us to understand that she could play the part all by herself and on many occasions would take quite a different line from his.*]
Heavens, Lamberto, just for a member of his staff?

LAUDISI

Member of his staff? In the Government Building, yes. But not at home!

DINA

[*Nineteen years old. Has a certain air of understanding everything better than her mother or her father. But this air is softened by considerable youthful charm.*]
But he's come here and put his mother-in-law in an apartment right next to ours—on our floor!

LAUDISI

Wasn't he entitled to? There was an apartment for rent,
so he rented it for his mother-in-law. [*Petulant, laying
it on thick*] Or do you think the old lady should have
asked your permission? Just because your father is
above her son-in-law at the office?

AMALIA

What do you mean? As a matter of fact, Dina and I
took the initiative and went to visit her first. [*With
emphasis*] She didn't receive us.

LAUDISI

And now what's your husband gone running to the
Governor for? Is he appealing to the authorities? To
force them into an act of courtesy?

AMALIA

Into an act of just reparation anyway! You don't leave
two ladies standing at the door like a couple of posts.

LAUDISI

What a pompous attitude! Aren't people allowed to
stay home and enjoy a little privacy?

AMALIA

All right, if you don't wish to realize that we were the
ones who tried to be courteous to a stranger. We went
to her first.

DINA

Now really, Uncle, be sensible! If you like we'll be
frank and admit it: we were courteous out of curiosity.
But, come, isn't that natural?

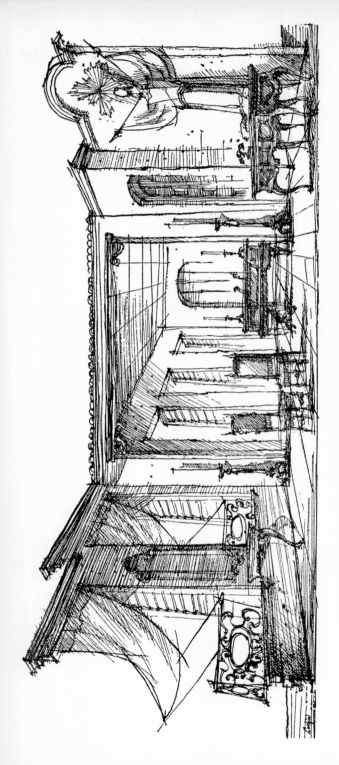

Sketch by Peter Larkin for the Westport production

LAUDISI

Natural, by all means: you've all got nothing to do.

DINA

Now, look, Uncle. There you stand minding your own
business. Taking no notice what other people are doing. Good. I come into the room. And there—on the
little table just in front of you—cool as a cucumber, or
rather with a long face like that jailbird we were talking about—I set down—well, what?—let's say a pair
of the cook's shoes.

LAUDISI

[*Impatiently*]
What have the cook's shoes to do with it?

DINA

[*Quickly*]
Ha, you see? You're amazed. You find it queer and at
once ask the why and wherefore.

LAUDISI

[*Pauses, smiles coldly, speedily recovers*]
What a girl! Pretty bright, aren't you? But you're talking with me, don't forget. You come and put the cook's
shoes on the table just to awaken my curiosity. Obvi-
ously—since you did it with this in mind—you can't
reproach me if I ask: "But *why* are the cook's shoes
here on the table, my dear?" Just as you have to show
me that this Signor Ponza—rascal and boor as your
father calls him—*intentionally* found an apartment
for his mother-in-law here in this house.

DINA

All right. Let's suppose it wasn't intentional. You can't
deny that the strange way the man lives would be bound
to arouse the curiosity of the whole town, it's only natural. Think. He arrives. He finds a place to live on
the top floor of that murky tenement, the one on the
edge of town, looking out on the orchards . . . Have
you seen it? Inside, I mean?

LAUDISI

You've been to see it?

DINA

Yes, Uncle. With Mother. And we're not the only ones
either. Everybody's been to see it. There's a courtyard,
and is it dark! Like a well. Way up on the top floor
there's a balcony with an iron railing. They let baskets
down from it on ropes.

LAUDISI

What of it?

DINA

[*With amazement and indignation*]
That's where he's put his wife: up there.

AMALIA

While he puts his mother-in-law here—next door to
us.

LAUDISI

In a nice apartment with a central location. Lucky
mother-in-law!

AMALIA

Lucky? He's just compelling her to live apart from her daughter!

LAUDISI

Who told you? Couldn't it be her own idea? She may want more freedom.

DINA

What nonsense, Uncle! Everyone knows it's his idea.

AMALIA

Now look. Everyone understands a daughter leaving her mother's house when she gets married—and going to live with her husband—in another city, if necessary. But you don't mean to say you understand it if a mother—unable to bear being away from the daughter —follows her and then is compelled to live apart from her in a city where after all *she's* a stranger too?

LAUDISI

Why not? Have you no imagination? Is it so hard to suppose that through her fault, or his, or nobody's, there might be some . . . incompatibility of charac- ter through which, even in those conditions . . .

DINA

[*Interrupting, amazed*]
What, Uncle? Between mother and daughter?

LAUDISI

Why between mother and daughter?

AMALIA

Because it couldn't be the other two, they're always together.

DINA

It's true. To everyone's astonishment, husband and mother-in-law are always together.

AMALIA

He comes here every evening—to keep her company.

DINA

Even in the day he usually comes over a couple of times.

LAUDISI

You suspect they make love maybe—husband and mother-in-law?

DINA

Uncle! How can you speak so of a poor old lady?

AMALIA

He never brings her daughter. Never, never, never does he bring his wife to her own mother!

LAUDISI

She must be sick, poor girl, and can't go out of doors . . .

DINA

Nonsense. The mother goes there . . .

AMALIA

She goes, yes, just to look on from a distance! Everyone knows the poor mother isn't allowed to go up to
the daughter's apartment.

DINA

She can only talk to her from the courtyard below.

AMALIA

From the courtyard, understand?

DINA

While her daughter is up there on the balcony—in the
sky practically! The poor old thing enters the courtyard, pulls the rope, the bell rings up above, the daughter comes out on the balcony, and the old lady talks
to her, from the bottom of that well, stretching her
neck back like this. Imagine! She doesn't even see her,
she's blinded by the sunlight pouring down from
above.

[*There is a knock at the door and the Butler ap-
pears.*]

Scene 2

THE SAME, THE BUTLER, *then* SIGNORA SIRELLI,
SIGNOR SIRELLI, SIGNORA CINI

BUTLER

Are you at home, Signora?

AMALIA

Who is it?

BUTLER

Signor Sirelli, Signora Sirelli, and another lady, Signora.

AMALIA

Very well, show them in.
  [*The Butler bows and leaves.*]

AMALIA

  [*To Signora Sirelli*]
How are you, my dear?

SIGNORA SIRELLI

  [*Fattish, red-faced, still young, dressed with exaggerated provincial elegance, burning with restless curiosity; harsh to her husband*]
I've ventured to bring my good friend Signora Cini who *so* much wanted to meet you!

AMALIA

How are you, Signora? Do sit down, everybody. [*Making the introductions*] This is my daughter, Dina. My brother, Lamberto Laudisi.

SIRELLI

  [*Bald, around forty, fat, with oiled hair and much pretense of elegant dress, squeaking, shiny shoes. Bowing*]
Signora! Signorina! [*Shaking Laudisi's hand*]

SIGNORA SIRELLI

Ah, dear Signora, we come here as to the fountain, two poor women *athirst* for news!

AMALIA

News of what, ladies?

SIGNORA SIRELLI

Why, of this blessed new secretary in the Government Building. No one in town talks of anything else!

SIGNORA CINI

[*An old fool, full of greedy malice veiled beneath an air of naïveté*]
We feel such curiosity about it, such curiosity!

AMALIA

But we don't know any more about it than you, believe me, Signora!

SIRELLI

[*To his wife, as if scoring a triumph*]
What did I tell you? They don't know any more than me, maybe less. [*Turning to the others*] The reason why this poor mother can't go and visit her daughter, for example—do you know what it really is?

AMALIA

I was just speaking of it with my brother.

LAUDISI

In whose opinion you've all gone mad!

DINA

[*Quickly, so as to ignore Laudisi*]
Because the husband—so they say—forbids her to.

SIGNORA CINI

[*In a tone of lamentation*]
Not enough of a reason, Signorina.

SIGNORA SIRELLI

[*Pressing the issue*]
Not nearly enough, there's more to it!

SIRELLI

[*With a gesture to attract attention*]
A piece of news for you, hot off the griddle. [*Emphasizing every syllable*] He keeps her under lock and key!

AMALIA

Whom? His mother-in-law?

SIRELLI

No, Signora. His wife!

SIGNORA SIRELLI

His wife, his wife!

SIGNORA CINI

[*In a tone of lamentation*]
Under lock and key!

DINA

You understand, Uncle? You who wish to excuse—

SIRELLI

[*Astonished*]
What? You'd want to excuse this monster?

LAUDISI

But I don't wish to excuse him in the least! I say that
your curiosity—begging all your pardons—is insufferable—if only because it is useless.

SIRELLI

Useless?

LAUDISI

Useless! Useless, good ladies!

SIGNORA CINI

Useless? To try and find out?

LAUDISI

Find out what, if I may ask? What can we really know
of other people, who they are, what they are, what
they are doing, why they are doing it—

SIGNORA SIRELLI

By demanding news, information—

LAUDISI

If anyone should be abreast of all the news, that person
is you, Signora—with a husband like yours, always
informed of everything!

SIRELLI

[*Trying to interrupt*]
Excuse me—

SIGNORA SIRELLI

No, no, my dear: I admit it's the truth! [*Turning to*

Amalia] The truth, my dear, is that, with a husband who always claims to know *every*thing, I never manage to know *any*thing!

SIRELLI

No wonder! She's never satisfied with what I tell her. Always suspects that a thing is not as I have said. Maintains, as a matter of fact, that it *can't* be as I have said. And in the end decides it must be exactly the opposite.

SIGNORA SIRELLI

Now just a minute, if you come and tell me—

LAUDISI

[*Laughs aloud*]
May I say something, Signora? I will answer your husband. My dear man, how do you expect your wife to be satisfied with the things you tell her if you—as is natural—present them as they are to you?

SIGNORA SIRELLI

As they absolutely cannot be!

LAUDISI

Ah no, Signora, permit me to say that now *you* are in the wrong! To your husband, rest assured, things are as he tells you they are!

SIRELLI

They are what they *really* are, what they *really* are!

SIGNORA SIRELLI

Not in the least. You are always wrong!

SIRELLI

You are wrong, I beg you to believe. *I* am right!

LAUDISI

No, no, my dear friends. Neither of you is wrong. May I explain? I'll prove it to you. [*He rises and goes to the middle of the room.*] Both of you see me? You do see me, don't you?

SIRELLI

Why, of course.

LAUDISI

No, no, don't speak too quickly, my friend. Come here!

SIRELLI

[*Looks at him, smiles, perplexed and a little disconcerted, not wishing to lend himself to a joke he doesn't understand*]
What for?

SIGNORA SIRELLI

[*Pushing him. Her voice is irritable.*]
Go on.

LAUDISI

[*To Sirelli who has now approached, trembling*]
You see me? Take a better look. Touch me.

SIGNORA SIRELLI

[*To her husband, who still hesitates to touch him*]
Touch him!

LAUDISI

[*To Sirelli, who has raised one hand with which he gingerly touches his shoulder*]
That's it, well done. You're sure you touch me—just as you see me—isn't that so?

SIRELLI

I'd say so.

LAUDISI

You can't doubt it, of course. Go back to your seat.

SIGNORA SIRELLI

[*To her husband who has remained in front of Laudisi, stupified*]
It's no use standing there blinking, go and sit down!

LAUDISI

[*To Signora Sirelli, now that her husband has gone back, still in a stupor, to his seat*]
Now would *you* like to come, Signora? [*Quickly, before she can move*] No, no, I'll come to you. [*He is now before her, down on one knee.*] You see me, don't you? Raise one little hand, touch me. [*And as Signora Sirelli, still seated, places one hand on his shoulder, bending down to kiss it*] Dear little hand!

SIRELLI

[*Warningly*]
Uh, uh.

LAUDISI

Take no notice of him. Are you, too, certain that you touch me just as you see me? You can't doubt it, can

you? But I beg you, don't tell your husband, or my
sister, or my niece, or this lady here, Signora——

SIGNORA CINI

[*Prompting*]
Cini.

LAUDISI

Cini. Don't tell them *what* you see in me, because all
four will tell you you are wrong, whereas you are not
wrong in the least: I really am as you see me. But,
dear lady, that doesn't stop me really being as your
husband sees me, as my sister sees me, as my niece
sees me, as this lady here, Signora——

SIGNORA CINI

[*Prompting*]
Cini.

LAUDISI

Cini sees me——for they aren't wrong either.

SIGNORA SIRELLI

How's that? You're a different person for each one of
us?

LAUDISI

Certainly I am, dear lady, aren't you?

SIGNORA SIRELLI

[*In a rush*]
No, no, no, no, no! As I see it, I'm myself and that's
that.

LAUDISI

As *I* see it, I'm *my*self and that's that. And if you people don't see me as I see myself, I say you're wrong— but this is all so much presumption—in me or in you, dear lady.

SIRELLI

May I ask what you hope to conclude with all this hocus-pocus?

LAUDISI

You think there's no conclusion to be drawn? Well, well. You're all so anxious to find out who other people are and what things are like, almost as if people and things were simply this way or that way.

SIGNORA SIRELLI

According to you, then, one can never know the truth?

SIGNORA CINI

Why, if seeing and touching aren't believing . . .

LAUDISI

But they are, dear lady, rest assured! All I'm saying is: respect what other people see and touch even if it's the opposite of what *you* see and touch!

SIGNORA SIRELLI

Listen to him! I turn my back on you, I won't talk with you any more. I don't want to go mad.

LAUDISI

Well, that's enough then. Go on talking of Signora

Frola and Signor Ponza, her son-in-law. I won't interrupt again.

AMALIA

God be praised! You'd do even better, my dear Lamberto, if you would leave us.

DINA

Yes, leave us, Uncle, do, do!

LAUDISI

Why should I? It amuses me to hear you talk. I'll keep
my mouth shut, don't worry. At the most I'll permit
myself a quiet smile—and if I actually burst out
laughing you'll just have to excuse me.

SIGNORA SIRELLI

And to think that we had come to find out . . . ! Now,
Signora, isn't your husband above this Signor Ponza
in the office?

AMALIA

The office is one thing, the home another, Signora.

SIGNORA SIRELLI

That's right, I understand! But haven't you even tried
to see his mother-in-law who lives here?

DINA

Oh yes, Signora. Twice.

SIGNORA CINI

[*With a start; then, with greedy, intent concentra-
tion*]
Ah! So you *have* talked to her?

AMALIA

She didn't receive us, my dear.

SIRELLI, SIGNORA SIRELLI, SIGNORA CINI

Oh!!! How is that possible?

DINA

We went there this morning for the second time—

AMALIA

The first time we waited more than a quarter of an hour at the door. Nobody came to open it, we couldn't so much as leave a visiting card. Today we tried again—

DINA

[*With a gesture of horror*]
And *he* came to the door!

SIGNORA SIRELLI

That face of his! There's something *bad* in it. It's a public menace, the whole town is affected. Then the way he dresses, always in black . . . All three of them wear black, his wife too—the old lady's daughter —isn't that so?

SIRELLI

[*With annoyance*]
You know that no one has even seen the old lady's daughter! I've told you a thousand times. One *supposes* she wears black . . . They're from a village in Marsica—

AMALIA

Yes, totally destroyed, it seems—

SIRELLI

Razed to the ground in the last earthquake.

DINA

I heard they lost all their relatives.

SIGNORA CINI

[*Anxious to take up the interrupted discussion*]
Yes, yes—so, *he* came to the door?

AMALIA

The moment I saw him in front of me with that face
of his I was struck dumb. I couldn't even find the
words to say we'd come to call on his mother-in-law.
He said nothing either! Didn't even thank me.

DINA

Oh, well, he did bow!

AMALIA

Only just: he nodded his head like this.

DINA

His eyes spoke, though, didn't they? They're a wild
beast's eyes, not a man's.

SIGNORA CINI

[*As above*]
What next? What did he say next?

DINA

He was very embarrassed—

AMALIA

And very dishevelled. He told us his mother-in-law was
not well, that he wanted to thank us for our courtesy,
then he just stood there in the doorway waiting for us
to go!

DINA

What a humiliation!

SIRELLI

He's a boor. Oho, you can be sure *he's* at the bottom of
the whole thing. Maybe he has his mother-in-law under lock and key too!

SIGNORA SIRELLI

The nerve of the man! To behave like that to a lady—
the wife of a superior!

AMALIA

This time my husband really got indignant. He said
the fellow was gravely lacking in respect and off he's
gone to make a strong protest to the Governor and demand satisfaction.

DINA

Oh good, here *is* Father!

Scene 3

THE SAME, COUNCILLOR AGAZZI

AGAZZI

Fifty, red hair, untidy, with beard, gold-rimmed glasses; an air of authority and malevolence.
My dear Sirelli. [*He approaches, bows, and shakes hands with Signora Sirelli.*] Signora.

AMALIA

[*Introducing him to Signora Cini*]
My husband—Signora Cini.

AGAZZI

[*Bows, shakes hands*]
Delighted. [*He then turns, almost solemnly, to his wife and daughter.*] I have to report that Signora Frola will be here at any moment.

SIGNORA SIRELLI

[*Clapping her hands, exultant*]
Really? She'll be here?

AGAZZI

It had to be done. Could I tolerate such a glaring misdemeanor towards my home, towards my women folk?

SIRELLI

Quite so. Just what we were saying.

SIGNORA SIRELLI

And it would be good to take this opportunity—

AGAZZI

[*Anticipating*]
To notify the Governor of everything the town is saying
in regard to this gentleman? Don't worry, I've done so!

SIRELLI

Oh, good, good!

SIGNORA CINI

Such *inexplicable* things! Absolutely *inconceivable!*

AMALIA

Positively *wild!* Do you know he keeps them under
lock and key—both of them!

DINA

Well, Mother, we don't know about the mother-in-law
yet.

SIGNORA SIRELLI

It's certain about his wife, though!

SIRELLI

What about the Governor?

AGAZZI

Yes, the Governor . . . well . . . it made a profound impression on him . . .

SIRELLI

That's good.

AGAZZI

Something had got through to him too, of course, and

now, like the rest of us, he sees how advisable it is to clear up this mystery. To find out the truth.

[*Laudisi laughs aloud.*]

AMALIA

The only thing missing in the picture: Lamberto laughing!

AGAZZI

What's he found to laugh at this time?

SIGNORA SIRELLI

He says it's not possible to discover the truth!

Scene 4

THE SAME, THE BUTLER, *then* SIGNORA FROLA

BUTLER

[*Comes to the doorway and announces*]
A visitor, Signora. Signora Frola.

SIRELLI

Ah! Here she is.

AGAZZI

We'll soon see if it's possible to discover the truth, my dear Lamberto.

SIGNORA SIRELLI

Wonderful! Oh, I'm so glad!

Impression by Lester Polakov of the Brattle Theatre production

AMALIA

[*Rising, to Agazzi*]
Shall we have her come in?

AGAZZI

Yes, yes, show her in. But let's set the stage. Move your
chairs back a little, will you? That's it. Now sit down,
I beg you. Wait till she arrives. We should all be
seated. Seated.
[*The Butler withdraws. After a brief pause Signora
Frola enters and all rise. Signora Frola is an old lady,
neat, unpretentious, very affable; with a great sadness
in her eyes, softened by the sweet smile that is con-
stantly on her lips. Amalia goes forward and extends
her hand.*]

AMALIA

Come in, Signora. [*Holding her hand, she introduces
her.*] Signora Cini. Signora Sirelli, my good friend.
Signor Sirelli. My husband. My daughter, Dina. My
brother, Lamberto Laudisi. Please sit down, Signora.

SIGNORA FROLA

I'm most distressed. I've come to beg pardon for having neglected my duty till today. It was so gracious of
you, Signora, to honor me with a visit when it was
for me to be the first to come.

AMALIA

Among neighbors, Signora, we take no notice whose
turn comes first. Especially since you're alone here
and strange to the neighborhood, we thought you might
be in need . . .

SIGNORA FROLA

Thank you, thank you . . . you are too kind . . .

SIGNORA SIRELLI

You are alone in our town, Signora?

SIGNORA FROLA

No, I have a married daughter. She came here too not long ago.

SIRELLI

The Signora's son-in-law is a secretary in the Government Building—Signor Ponza—isn't that so?

SIGNORA FROLA

That's right, yes. And I do hope Councillor Agazzi will excuse me . . . and my son-in-law too . . .

AGAZZI

To tell you the truth, Signora, I did take it rather ill—

SIGNORA FROLA

[*Interrupting*]
You were right, quite right! But you must excuse him! Believe me when I say we are still overwhelmed by . . . what happened.

AMALIA

Of course, you were in that terrible disaster!

SIGNORA SIRELLI

You lost relatives?

SIGNORA FROLA

All of them—all, Signora. There isn't a trace of our village left. Just a heap of ruins with fields all round. Deserted.

SIRELLI

Just what we heard.

SIGNORA FROLA

I only had a sister—and her daughter, unmarried luckily . . . But it was a much harder blow for my poor son-in-law: mother, two brothers, a sister, the brothers' wives, the sister's husband, two nephews . . .

SIRELLI

A massacre!

SIGNORA FROLA

Blows you can never recover from. It's like being— stunned.

AMALIA

It certainly is.

SIGNORA SIRELLI

And all from one moment to the next. It's enough to drive people mad.

SIGNORA FROLA

Your mind doesn't work, you forget and overlook things without in the least meaning to, Councillor.

AGAZZI

Please, Signora, not a word of excuse!

AMALIA

This terrible . . . blow was one of the reasons my daughter and I came to see you . . . first.

SIGNORA SIRELLI

[*Writhing with curiosity*]
That's right. They knew how alone you were! Though . . . excuse me, Signora, for wondering how it is . . . with your daughter here . . . . after such a blow . . . that . . . [*After this enterprising start she is suddenly bashful.*] . . . it seems to me that survivors would feel the need to stand together—

SIGNORA FROLA

[*Continuing, to save her from embarrassment*]
How it is that I am quite alone?

SIRELLI

Exactly! It does seem strange—to be frank with you.

SIGNORA FROLA

[*Distressed*]
Yes, I understand. [*Then, trying a possible way out*] But—when your son or your daughter gets married, it's my opinion they should be left to themselves—to make their own life, that's all.

LAUDISI

How right you are! And this life must be a new life, revealing itself in the new relationship with wife or husband.

SIGNORA SIRELLI

But not to the extent, my dear Laudisi, of excluding the mother's life from her own!

LAUDISI

Who talked of exclusion? We are talking now, if I understand the matter, of a mother who sees that her daughter neither can nor should stay tied to her as she was before—because now she has a life of her own.

SIGNORA FROLA

[*With keen gratitude*]
That's it, that's how it is, ladies! Thank you, that's exactly what I was trying to say.

SIGNORA CINI

But I'm sure your daughter *does* come—does come quite often—to keep you company?

SIGNORA FROLA

[*Uncomfortable*]
Surely . . . of course . . . we see each other, naturally . . .

SIRELLI

[*Promptly*]
Yet your daughter never goes out—at any rate no one has ever seen her!

SIGNORA CINI

Perhaps she has children to look after?

SIGNORA FROLA

[*Promptly*]

No. There are no children yet. And maybe she will never have any—now. She's been married seven years. She has things to do in the house, of course. But that isn't it. [*She smiles in her distress, adding, as another possible way of escape*] In small towns we're used to staying home all the time, we women are used to it.

AGAZZI

Even when there's a mother for us to go and see? A mother who doesn't live with us any more?

AMALIA

But the Signora does go to see her daughter, doesn't she?

SIGNORA FROLA

[*Promptly*]

Certainly. Oh, yes! I go once or twice a day.

SIRELLI

You climb all those stairs twice a day—to the top floor of that tenement?

SIGNORA FROLA

[*Growing pale, still trying to turn the torture of this questioning into a smile*]

No, it's true I don't go up, you're right, ladies, they'd be too many for me, the stairs. I don't go up. My daughter comes to the balcony in the courtyard and—we see each other, we talk.

SIGNORA SIRELLI

Only that way? You never see her close up?

DINA

[*With her arm around her mother's neck*]
As a daughter, I don't claim my mother would climb
ninety or a hundred stairs for me, but I wouldn't be
satisfied with seeing her, with talking to her from a
distance, without embracing her, without feeling her
near me.

SIGNORA FROLA

[*Keenly disturbed, embarrassed*]
You are right. Oh, well, I see I have to speak out. I
wouldn't like you to think something of my daughter
that is not the case—that she isn't fond of me, isn't considerate toward me. As for myself—I'm her mother—
ninety or a hundred stairs wouldn't keep a mother
away, even if she *is* old and tired, when such a prize
awaits her at the top, and she can press her daughter
to her heart.

SIGNORA SIRELLI

[*Triumphant*]
Aha! Just what we said, Signora! There must be a reason!!

AMALIA

[*Pointedly*]
You see, Lamberto: there *is* a reason!

SIRELLI

[*Promptly*]
Your son-in-law, eh?

SIGNORA FROLA

Oh dear, please, please, don't think ill of him! He's such a fine young fellow. You can't imagine how kind he is—what tender and delicate affection he shows me —how much attention he pays me! To say nothing of the loving care he lavishes on my daughter! Believe me, I couldn't have wished her a better husband!

SIGNORA SIRELLI

But . . . in that case . . .

SIGNORA CINI

He can't be the reason!

AGAZZI

Of course not. It doesn't seem to me *possible* he should forbid his wife to go and see her mother—or her mother to come and be with *her* a little!

SIGNORA FROLA

Forbid? But I never said he forbade it. It's ourselves, Councillor, my daughter and I: we do without each other's company—of our own accord, believe me— for his sake.

AGAZZI

But how, pray, could he take offense? I don't see it.

SIGNORA FROLA

It's not a matter of offense, Councillor. It's a feeling . . . a feeling, ladies, rather hard to understand. But when you do understand it, it's not hard—to sympa-

thize—although it may mean we have to make a real
sacrifice, my daughter and I.

AGAZZI

At least you must admit it's *strange,* what you have to
tell us, Signora.

SIRELLI

It certainly is. It arouses, and justifies, curiosity.

AGAZZI

Curiosity—and suspicion.

SIGNORA FROLA

Against him? Please, please don't say that! *What*
could anyone suspect, Councillor?

AGAZZI

Nothing at all. Don't be disturbed. I'm saying that
suspicion *could* arise.

SIGNORA FROLA

Oh no, no! *What* can they suspect, if we are in perfect
agreement? My daughter and I are satisfied, completely satisfied!

SIGNORA SIRELLI

He's jealous, perhaps?

SIGNORA FROLA

Jealous of her mother? I don't think you could call it
that. Though, of course, I can't claim to know. Look,
he wants his wife's heart all to himself. He admits my

daughter loves me too, must love me, he fully and gladly admits it, but he wants her love to come to me through him, *he* wants to bring it to me.

AGAZZI

No, I don't see. If you'll forgive me, I consider it the purest cruelty, behavior like that.

SIGNORA FROLA

Cruelty!! No, NO!! Don't call it cruelty, Councillor, it's something else, believe me. I don't know how to put it into words. . . . His *nature,* that's it. Or— maybe—maybe it's a kind of—illness, call it that. It's —it's the fullness of his love, a love entire, exclusive. She must live shut up in it. With no doors: she mustn't go out and no one else must come in.

DINA

Not even her mother?

SIRELLI

Sheer selfishness I call that!

SIGNORA FROLA

Perhaps. But a selfishness that gives itself utterly and provides a world to live in—for his own wife. After all it would be selfishness on my part, were I to force my way into this closed world of love—when my daughter is happy within it. Happy and adored. To a mother, la- dies, that should be enough, shouldn't it? For the rest, if I see her, if I talk to my daughter . . . [*With a graceful, confidential movement*] The little basket in the courtyard carries a few words up to her, and a few

words back to me . . . our letters give the day's news.
I'm satisfied with that. And by this time I'm used to it
—I'm resigned, you might say. It doesn't hurt me now.

AMALIA

Well, of course, if you're both satisfied, you and your
daughter . . .

SIGNORA FROLA

[*Rising*]
We are, we are! Because he's so kind, believe me! He
couldn't be more so. We all have our weaknesses, **don't**
we? and we need each other's sympathy. [*Taking her
leave of Amalia*] Signora. [*Taking her leave first of
Signora Cini, Signora Sirelli, Sirelli, then turning to
Councillor Agazzi*] You *will* excuse me, won't you?

AGAZZI

Don't mention it, my dear Signora. We are most grateful for your visit.

SIGNORA FROLA

[*Nods to Dina and Laudisi, then turns to Amalia*]
Please **don't**—just stay here—please don't come to the
door.

AMALIA

Why, of course I will, it's my duty, Signora.
    [*Signora Frola leaves the room with Amalia, who
returns a moment later.*]

SIRELLI

Well, well, **well**! Are you satisfied with the explanation?

AGAZZI

What explanation? It seems to me everything is still shrouded in mystery.

SIGNORA SIRELLI

And who knows how much this poor soul of a mother must suffer!

DINA

Her daughter too, poor thing.
  [*Pause*]

SIGNORA CINI

[*From the corner of the room whither she has retired to hide her tears, with a strident explosion*]
She was nearly crying, the whole time!

AMALIA

I noticed it when she said she'd climb far more than a hundred stairs just to press her daughter to her heart!

LAUDISI

I thought she was trying to protect her son-in-law from suspicion. That seemed to be the whole aim of her visit.

SIGNORA SIRELLI

Not at all. Why, heavens, she had no idea how to excuse what he has done!

SIRELLI

Excuse? Excuse violence? Excuse downright barbarism?

Scene 5

THE SAME, THE BUTLER, *then* PONZA

BUTLER

[*Coming to the doorway*]
Signor Agazzi, Signor Ponza is here. He wishes to be
received.

SIGNORA SIRELLI

Ah! That man!!
[*General surprise. A movement of anxious curiosity, almost of dismay*]

AGAZZI

He wants *me* to receive him?

BUTLER

Yes, Signore, that's what he says.

SIGNORA SIRELLI

Oh please, Councillor, receive him, receive him *here!*
I'm almost afraid, but I'm so curious to see him close
up! The monster!!

AMALIA

What does he want?

AGAZZI

Let's find out. Show him in. Be seated, everybody. We
must all be seated!
[*The Butler bows and withdraws. A moment's
pause. Enter Ponza. Thickset, dark, almost fierce-*

looking, clad all in black, thick black hair, low fore-head, big black moustache. He keeps clenching his fists, speaks with an effort, with barely suppressed vio-lence. From time to time he wipes his sweat off with a black-bordered handkerchief. When he speaks his eyes stay hard, fixed, dismal.]
Come in, come right in, Signor Ponza. [*Introducing him*] The new executive secretary: Signor Ponza. My wife—Signora Sirelli—Signora Cini—my daughter —Signor Sirelli—my brother-in-law, Laudisi. Please sit down.

PONZA

Thank you. I'll only be troubling you for a moment.

AGAZZI

Would you like to speak with me in private?

PONZA

No, I can—I can speak in front of everybody. It's bet-ter that way. The declaration I have to make is a matter of duty—*my* duty—

AGAZZI

You mean about your mother-in-law's not visiting us? You really needn't bother, because—

PONZA

It's not that, Councillor. I feel I must tell you my mother-in-law, Signora Frola, would undoubtedly have come to visit you before your wife and daughter had the goodness to come to her, had I not done all I could to prevent her doing so. I couldn't permit her either to pay visits or to receive them.

AGAZZI

[*With pride and resentment*]
And why not, may I ask?

PONZA

[*Getting more excited all the time despite his ef-
forts to control himself*]
I suppose my mother-in-law has been talking to you
all? Has told you I forbid her to enter my home and
see her daughter?

AMALIA

No, no! She was full of consideration and kindness
toward you.

DINA

She had nothing but good to say of you.

AGAZZI

She said she refrains from entering her daughter's
home of her own accord, out of respect for a feeling of
yours which we frankly admit we don't understand.

SIGNORA SIRELLI

In fact if we were to say what we really think of it . . .

AGAZZI

Yes. It seemed to us a piece of cruelty. Real cruelty.

PONZA

I came here expressly to clear this up, Councillor. This
lady's condition is a pitiful one, but my own is scarcely
less pitiful. For I see I am obliged to beg pardon, I am

obliged to tell you all about a misfortune which—
which only such violence as this could compel me to
reveal. [*He stops a moment to look at everyone. Then,
in a slow and staccato voice*] Signora Frola is mad.

EVERYONE

[*Jumping out of his skin*]
Mad?

PONZA

She's been mad for four years.

SIGNORA SIRELLI

[*With a cry*]
Heavens, she doesn't *seem* mad!

AGAZZI

[*Stunned*]
What? Mad?

PONZA

She doesn't *seem* mad, but she *is* mad. And her madness consists precisely in believing that I don't wish
her to see her daughter. [*With terrible excitement, almost ferocious perturbation*] And what daughter, in
heaven's name? Her daughter died four years ago.

EVERYONE

[*Flabbergasted*]
Died? Oh! What? Died?

PONZA

Four years ago. That's what drove her mad.

SIRELLI

Then, the lady who is your wife today?

PONZA

I married again. Two years ago.

AMALIA

And the old lady thinks your present wife is her daughter?

PONZA

Such has been her good fortune, one might almost say. She was under surveillance, not allowed to go out. But one day, through her window, she saw me in the street with my second wife. She thought it was her daughter, still alive. She started laughing, trembling all over. At a single blow she was free of the dark desperation she had fallen into—only to find herself in another insanity. At first she was exultant, ecstatic. Then, bit by bit, she grew calmer and, despite the anguish in her heart, managed to subside into an attitude of resignation. She is satisfied, as you could see. She persists in believing that her daughter is not dead but that I want to keep her all to myself and not let anyone see her. She seems quite cured. So much so that, to hear her talk, you wouldn't think she was mad in the least.

AMALIA

Not in the least!

SIGNORA SIRELLI

It's true, she does say she's satisfied now.

PONZA

She tells everyone that. And is grateful and affectionate to me. Because I try to back her up in every possible
way, even if it means heavy sacrifices. I have to maintain two households. I oblige my wife—who, luckily,
complies in the spirit of charity—to confirm the illusion of being her daughter. She comes to the window,
talks to her, writes to her. But—well, my friends, there
are human limits to charity, to duty. I can't compel my
wife to live with her. In the meanwhile she lives in a
prison, poor woman, I have to lock her up—for fear
she might one day climb those stairs and knock on our
door. Yes, she is peaceful now, and of a gentle dispo-
sition in any case, but you will understand how
my wife would feel were the old lady to shower
motherly caresses on her. She'd shudder from head
to foot.

AMALIA

[*With a start: horror and pity mixed*]
Oh, of course! Poor lady, just imagine!

SIGNORA SIRELLI

[*To her husband and Signora Cini*]
Ah, so she *wishes* to be under lock and key, did you
hear?

PONZA

[*Cutting her short*]
Councillor Agazzi, you will understand that I couldn't
have permitted this visit of my mother-in-law's—except that I had to.

AGAZZI

I understand perfectly. Yes, it's clear to me now.

PONZA

I know people should keep their misfortunes to themselves. But I was compelled to have my mother-in-law
come here. And I was obliged to make this declaration
of my own. With a position like mine to keep up. We
can't have the people in town believing a public official
would do such things. Believing he would keep a poor
mother from seeing her daughter. Out of jealousy or
anything else. [*Rises*] Councillor Agazzi. [*He bows.
Then passing Laudisi and Sirelli, he nods to them.*]
Gentlemen. [*He leaves.*]

AMALIA

[*In astonishment*]
Oh!! So she's mad!!!

SIGNORA SIRELLI

Poor lady: mad!

DINA

So that's it; she thinks herself still a mother, but that
woman isn't her daughter! [*Horrified, she buries her
face in her hands.*] Heavens!

SIGNORA CINI

Who could ever have guessed such a thing?

AGAZZI

Well, I don't know . . . from the way she talked—

LAUDISI

You knew all along?

AGAZZI

Not exactly . . . but it *is* true she—didn't quite know what to say.

SIGNORA SIRELLI

But that's only natural. She's lost her reason.

SIRELLI

I wonder, though. It's strange—for a mad woman. She wasn't very reasonable, certainly. But all this trying to explain why her son-in-law doesn't want to let her see her daughter. All this excusing of him and quickly adapting herself to her own improvisations of the moment . . .

AGAZZI

Gracious! That's precisely the proof that she's mad—the fact that she seeks excuses for her son-in-law without finding a single one that's halfway convincing.

AMALIA

Yes, yes. She was always saying things and then taking them back again.

AGAZZI

[*To Sirelli*]
D'you think anyone who wasn't mad could accept such conditions? To see her daughter only at the window—with the excuse she gives about the morbid love of the husband who wants his wife all to himself?

SIRELLI

I don't know. *Would* a madwoman accept such conditions? And resign herself to them? I find it strange,
very strange. [*To Laudisi*] What do you say?

LAUDISI

Me? Why, nothing.

Scene 6

THE SAME, THE BUTLER, *then* SIGNORA FROLA

BUTLER

[*Knocking, then appearing in the doorway, excited*]
Excuse me, sir. Signora Frola is here again.

AMALIA

[*Upset*]
Heavens, what now? Shall we never be rid of her?

SIGNORA SIRELLI

Never be rid of her? Oh, you mean because she's mad
—I see.

SIGNORA CINI

Lord, Lord, who knows what she'll say this time? Still,
I'd like to hear it.

SIRELLI

I'm curious about it too. I'm not at all convinced she *is*
mad.

DINA

Look, Mother, there's nothing to be afraid of. She's so calm.

AGAZZI

We must receive her, of course. Let's hear what it is she wants. If there's trouble, we can take care of it. But let's set the stage. And be seated, everybody. We must all be seated. [*To the Butler*] Show her in.
[*The Butler withdraws.*]

AMALIA

Help me, all of you, please! I don't know how to talk to her now.
[*Signora Frola re-enters. Amalia rises and comes towards her, frightened. The others look on in dismay.*]

SIGNORA FROLA

Excuse me.

AMALIA

Come in, come right in, Signora. My friends are still here, as you see—

SIGNORA FROLA

[*With very mournful affability, smiling*]
The look you all give me . . . you too, dear Signora, you think I'm a poor madwoman, don't you?

AMALIA

Why, no, Signora, what are you saying?

SIGNORA FROLA

[*With profound sorrow*]
The first time you came I didn't even go to the door, it
was better that way. I never thought you'd come again.
My son-in-law opened the door without thinking. So
you had called, and I had to return the visit. Alas, I
knew what the consequences would be!

AMALIA

Not at all, believe me. We're very pleased to see you
again.

SIRELLI

The Signora is troubled . . . we don't know why: let
her speak.

SIGNORA FROLA

Wasn't it my son-in-law who just left?

AGAZZI

Well, yes. He came—he came, Signora, to talk with
me about—office business, that's all.

SIGNORA FROLA

[*Wounded, with great consternation*]
That's a little white lie—you're saying it just to soothe
me down . . .

AGAZZI

No, no, Signora, be assured, I'm telling the truth.

SIGNORA FROLA

[*As above*]
At least he was calm? He talked calmly?

AGAZZI

Yes, yes, completely calm, wasn't he?
[*Everyone assents, confirms.*]

SIGNORA FROLA

Oh dear, you all think *you're* reassuring *me* whereas
what I want is to reassure you about him!

SIGNORA SIRELLI

On what score, Signora? If we repeat that—

AGAZZI

He spoke with me about some office business—

SIGNORA FROLA

I see how you all look at me! But wait. It's not a matter
of me at all. From the way you look at me I see that his
coming here has proved what I should never have revealed for all the gold in the world. You can all bear
witness that not long ago I didn't know what to reply
to your questions. Believe me, they hurt, they hurt very
much. And I gave you an explanation of this strange
way of living—an explanation that could satisfy no
one, I see that. But could I tell you the real reason?
Could I tell you the story he tells—that my daughter
died four years ago and that I'm a poor madwoman
who believes she's still alive and that he doesn't want
me to see her?

AGAZZI

[*Stunned by the profound note of sincerity in Signora Frola*]
Ah! What's this? Your daughter?

SIGNORA FROLA

[*Quickly, anxiously*]
You know it's true. Why try to hide it? That's what he
told you . . .

SIRELLI

[*Hesitating, but scrutinizing her*]
Yes . . . in fact . . . he did say . . .

SIGNORA FROLA

I know. And unhappily I know how it will stir him up
to feel compelled to say it of me. Our situation, Councillor, is one we've been able to handle—by ceaseless
effort, in the face of great suffering—but only this
way: by living as we are living. I quite understand how
it attracts attention, provokes scandal, arouses suspicion. On the other hand, he's a good worker, scrupu-
lous, conscientious—you must have tried him out already.

AGAZZI

Well, actually, I haven't had the chance to discover.

SIGNORA FROLA

Please don't judge from the way it looks now! He's
good—everyone he's ever worked for said so. So why
should he be tormented with an investigation of his
family life? I told you, Councillor: you're investigat-
ing a situation which is under control. To bring it out
in the open is simply to hurt him in his career.

AGAZZI

Signora, please don't distress yourself in this way! No
one wishes to torment him.

SIGNORA FROLA

Oh dear, how can I help being distressed when I see him compelled to give everybody an absurd explanation, a horrible explanation. Can you seriously believe that my daughter is dead? That I am mad? That his present wife is his second? But for him, it's a *necessity* to say it is so. Only in this way could he find peace and self-respect. Yet he himself admits the enormity of what he says. Whenever he's compelled to say it, he gets terribly excited, he's quite overcome—you must have noticed!

AGAZZI

Yes . . . in fact, he was . . . he was rather excited.

SIGNORA SIRELLI

Oh dear, what are we to make of it now? It's him?

SIRELLI

Of course. It must be. [*Triumphant*] My friends, I told you so!

AGAZZI

My God, is it possible?
  [*Much agitation all round*]

SIGNORA FROLA

[*Quickly, joining her hands*]
Please, please, good people! What are you thinking? It's only . . . he has one sore spot that mustn't be touched. Be reasonable: would I leave my daughter alone with him if he were really mad? No! You can test what I say at any time at the office, Councillor; you'll find he performs his duties to perfection!

AGAZZI

Well, Signora, you owe us an explanation—a clear explanation. Is it possible that your son-in-law came here and *invented* the whole story?

SIGNORA FROLA

Yes, Signore, it is. Let me explain it to you. But you must sympathize with him, Councillor.

AGAZZI

What? Then it isn't true that your daughter is dead?

SIGNORA FROLA

[*Horrified*]
Why no, heaven forbid!

AGAZZI

[*Very annoyed, shouting*]
Then it's he that's mad!

SIGNORA FROLA

[*Supplicating*]
No, no . . . look . . .

SIRELLI

[*Triumphant*]
But it must be, it must be!

SIGNORA FROLA

No, no, look! He's not mad. Let me speak. You've seen him: he has a strong constitution, he's violent. When he got married he was seized with a veritable frenzy of love. My daughter is so delicate, he came near to de-

stroying her—with the force of his passion. On the
advice of the doctors and all the relations—even his
(dead now, poor things!)—my daughter was taken off
in secret and shut up in a sanitarium. He was already
quite—exalted by excess of love, so when he couldn't
find her in the house, oh! my friends, he fell into such
a desperate state of mind. He *really* believed she was
dead. Would hear of nothing else. Wanted to wear
black. Did all sorts of crazy things. And wouldn't
budge from his idea. A year later, when my daughter
was well again, and blooming, and was brought back
to him, he said no, it wasn't she, no, no, he looked and
looked: it wasn't she. What torture, my friends! He
would go up to her, seem to recognize her, and then—
no, no! To induce him to take her, I got together with
his friends and we went through the pretense of a second wedding.

SIGNORA SIRELLI

Ah! So that's why he says . . .

SIGNORA FROLA

Yes, but for some time now he hasn't believed it himself. That's why he has to convince other people, he
can't help it. To relieve his own insecurity, you understand? For maybe, from time to time, the fear flashes
across his mind that his wife might be taken from him
again. [*In a lower tone, taking them into her confidence
with a smile*] That's why he keeps her under lock and
key, keeps her all to himself. But he adores her. I am
sure of it. And my daughter is satisfied. [*Rising*] Now
I must be going. I mustn't be here if he comes back
again in that excited state. [*She sighs sweetly, with a
movement of her joined hands.*] We must be patient.

That poor girl must pretend she's not herself but someone else, and I—I must pretend I'm mad, my friends!
What of it? As long as *he's* at peace. Please don't come
to the door. I know the way. Goodbye, goodbye!

[*Bowing and nodding to everyone, she hurriedly
withdraws. They all remain standing, looking at each
other, astounded, dumbfounded. Silence*]

LAUDISI

[*Coming center*]
You're looking each other over? The truth, hm?
[*He bursts out laughing.*]

Act II~Scene 1

When the curtain rises, AMALIA, DINA, *and* SIGNORA
SIRELLI *are talking in the music room. In the drawing
room are* AGAZZI, LAUDISI, *and* SIRELLI. *Agazzi is on
the phone, standing by his desk. Laudisi and Sirelli,
seated, are looking in his direction, waiting.*

AGAZZI

Hello. Yes. Is that Police Commissioner Centuri?
Well? Yes, fine. [*After listening for some time*] But
really, how is that possible? [*Another long wait*] I
quite understand, but if we could keep at it . . . [*Another
wait*] It's really very strange we can't . . .
[*Pause*] I see, yes, I see. [*Pause*] That'll do for now
then, we'll have to see . . . Goodbye. [*He puts down
the receiver and walks forward.*]

SIRELLI

[*Anxiously*]
Well?

AGAZZI

Nothing.

SIRELLI

They can't find anything at all?

AGAZZI

Everything's either dispersed or destroyed: the city
hall, the municipal archives, all records of births,
deaths, and marriages.

SIRELLI

But aren't there survivors who could give testimony?

AGAZZI

We've no news of any. And if there *are* some, it's going to be damned hard to find them at this point.

SIRELLI

So there's nothing for it but believing one or other of the two of them? Just that: no proofs, nothing.

AGAZZI

Unfortunately.

LAUDISI

[*Rising and drawing the curtains between the two rooms*]
Would you like to take *my* advice? Believe them both.

AGAZZI

Very well, and what if—

SIRELLI

What if one says black and the other says white?

LAUDISI

In that case, believe neither.

SIRELLI

You're trying to be funny. There may be no precise facts, the proofs may be missing, but the truth—the truth must be on one side or the other.

LAUDISI

Precise facts. Hm. What would you deduce from precise facts?

AGAZZI

Now, really. Take the daughter's death certificate—I mean if it's Signora Frola that's mad. It's true we can't find it, but then we can't find anything—yet it must have existed—and it might turn up tomorrow— and if it did—why, it'd be clear that *he's* in the right —the husband.

SIRELLI

Would you deny the validity of the evidence if you were given this certificate?

LAUDISI

I? I'm not denying anything. I'm very careful not to. It's you who feel the need of precise facts, documents and so forth. So you can affirm or deny. I wouldn't know what to do with them. For me reality isn't in *them*—it's in the two people, in the hearts of the two people. And how could *I* get into *their* hearts? All I know is what they tell me.

SIRELLI

Exactly. And doesn't each of them tell you the other is mad? Either *she's* mad or *he's* mad, there's no getting away from it. Well, which?

AGAZZI

That is the question.

LAUDISI

In the first place, it's not true each says the other is mad. Signor Ponza says Signora Frola is mad. She not only denies this, she denies that *he* is mad too. At worst,

she says, he was . . . "exalted with excess of love"
but that now he's completely well.

SIRELLI

Then you incline, as I do, toward *her* version of the
story?

AGAZZI

It's clear the whole thing can be satisfactorily explained on the basis of her statement.

LAUDISI

The whole thing can be satisfactorily explained on the
basis of his statement too.

SIRELLI

Then—neither of them is mad? But, damn it, one of
them *must* be!

LAUDISI

Then, which? You can't say. Nor can anyone else. And
this isn't just because your precise facts have been
wiped out—dispersed or destroyed—in some accident,
a fire or an earthquake. No, it's because they have
wiped them out in themselves, in their hearts. Do you
see that? She has created for him, or he for her, a
fantasy. This fantasy is as real as reality. And they're
living inside it now, with perfect harmony. They have
found peace there. They breathe and see and hear and
touch there. It is their reality, and no document could
conceivably destroy it. At best a document might do
you some good, it could satisfy your foolish curiosity.
But no document has turned up, so here you are faced
by two things—fantasy and reality—and you can't tell

the one from the other. That is your punishment. Marvellous, isn't it?

AGAZZI

That's just philosophy, my dear fellow. Wait. We'll
see if we can't get to the bottom of this.

SIRELLI

We've listened to him and we've listened to her. We
now put both stories together—confront one version
with the other—and figure out where fantasy begins,
where reality leaves off. Don't you think we'll succeed?

LAUDISI

All I ask is that you let me go on laughing when you've
finished.

AGAZZI

Well, well, we'll see who'll be laughing when we've
finished. Now let's lose no time. I have an idea! [*He
goes towards the music room and calls*] Amalia, Signora Sirelli, will you come in here now?

Scene 2

THE SAME, AMALIA, SIGNORA SIRELLI, DINA

SIGNORA SIRELLI

[*To Laudisi, threatening him with one finger*]
Still at it, you naughty man!

SIRELLI

He's incorrigible.

SIGNORA SIRELLI

Here we all are—in the grip of a mighty passion—determined to get to the heart of the mystery if we go mad in the process—I didn't sleep a wink last night, myself—and *you*, you are cold and indifferent?

AGAZZI

Please, Signora, simply ignore him. Just sit down all of you and pay attention to me.

LAUDISI

Yes, just pay attention to my brother-in-law. He's preparing you the best of sleeping pills for tonight.

AGAZZI

Well now, where were we? Oh, yes, my idea! You ladies will go to Signora Frola's . . .

AMALIA

But will she receive us?

AGAZZI

Oh yes, I think so.

DINA

It's our duty to return the visit.

AMALIA

But if he doesn't want to allow her to pay visits or receive them?

SIRELLI

That was before. When no one knew anything yet. But

now she's been forced to speak and in her own way
she's explained her reason for being so reserved . . .

SIGNORA SIRELLI

She may even enjoy speaking to us of her daughter.

DINA

She's so good-natured! *I* haven't a doubt in the world
—he's the one that's mad.

AGAZZI

Let's not rush the verdict. Now, er, listen to me a moment. [*He looks at the clock.*] Don't stay there long—a
quarter of an hour, not more.

SIRELLI

[*To his wife*]
Make a note of it.

SIGNORA SIRELLI

[*An angry outburst*]
May I ask *why* you say that to *me?*

SIRELLI

Why, because once you start talking—

DINA

[*Preventing a quarrel*]
A quarter of an hour: *I'll* make a note of it.

AGAZZI

I must go to the Government Building. I'll be back here
at eleven. That's not more than twenty minutes or so
from now.

SIRELLI

[*Fretting*]
What about me?

AGAZZI

Wait. [*To the women*] A little before eleven use some
pretext to get Signora Frola to come here.

AMALIA

Pretext—what pretext?

AGAZZI

Any pretext. You'll find one in the normal course of
conversation, won't you? Or are you women for nothing? You have Dina and Signora Sirelli to help you
. . . You'll bring her into the music room, of course.
[*He goes to the threshold of the music room.*] Now,
let's set the stage! These doors must be left open—
wide open like this—so we can hear you talking from
in here. On my desk I leave these papers, which I
should be taking with me. Office business—a brief spe-
cially prepared for Signor Ponza. I pretend to forget it
and so find an excuse to bring Ponza here.

SIRELLI

[*As above*]
What about me? Where do I come in? And when?

AGAZZI

When? Several minutes past eleven. When the ladies
are in the music room and I am here with him. You
come for your wife. Through that door. [*Pointing stage

left] I introduce you to Ponza as you're passing through
this room. Then I ask you to invite the ladies to join
us in here. When they all come in, Ponza will be sitting
here. I then put Signora Frola here. [*He indicates the
two ends of a little sofa.*] So they'll be side by side
and—

LAUDISI

We discover the truth!

DINA

Now really, Uncle, when the two of them meet face to
face—

AGAZZI

Take no notice of him, for heaven's sake! Go on, go on,
there isn't a moment to lose!

SIGNORA SIRELLI

Yes, let's be going, let's be going. [*To Laudisi*] I won't
shake hands with you!

LAUDISI

Then I'll do it for you, Signora. [*He shakes one hand
with the other.*] Good luck!
   [*Amalia, Dina and Signora Sirelli leave.*]

AGAZZI

[*To Sirelli*]
Shall we be going too, hm? Let's go.

SIRELLI

Yes, let's. Goodbye, Lamberto.

LAUDISI

Goodbye, goodbye.
  [*Agazzi and Sirelli leave.*]

Scene 3

LAUDISI, *then* THE BUTLER

LAUDISI

[*Walks round the room a bit, grinning to himself,
and nodding. Then he stops before the large mirror on
the mantelpiece, looks at his own reflection, and talks
to it.*]

Ah, so there you are! [*He waves at it with two fingers,
winks wickedly, and laughs sarcastically.*] Well, old
boy, which of us two is the madman? [*He raises one
hand and levels the index finger at his reflection which
in turn levels its index finger at him. Again the sarcas-
tic laugh*] Yes, I know: I say *you* and you point your
finger at *me*. Come now, between ourselves, we know
each other pretty well, the two of us. The only trouble
is, I see you one way and other people see you another
way. So what becomes of you, my dear fellow? Here
am I. I can touch myself. I can see myself. But what
can I make of you—the you that other people see, I
mean—what is it to me? I can't touch it. I can't see it.
In short, you're a creature of fantasy, a phantom, a
ghost! Well, you see *these* madmen? They're ghosts
too. But do they know it? Not in the least. "Let's set the
stage. Signor Ponza will be sitting here. I'll put Signora Frola here . . ." Driven by curiosity, they go

running after other ghosts—the Ponza *they* take him
to be, the Frola *they* take her to be—*other* ghosts are
something else again—

[*The Butler enters but stops in his tracks, astounded,
to hear Laudisi's last words. He then announces*]

BUTLER

Signor Lamberto.

LAUDISI

Uh?

BUTLER

There are two ladies here. Signora Cini and another.

LAUDISI

Do they want me?

BUTLER

They asked for the mistress, Signore. I said she'd gone
to visit Signora Frola next door and so . . .

LAUDISI

And so?

BUTLER

They looked at each other. Then they slapped their
little hands with their gloves. "Really?" they said,
"Really?" Then they asked very anxiously if there was
no one at all at home.

LAUDISI

And you said no one at all.

BUTLER

No, I said there was you, Signore.

LAUDISI

Me? Oh, no, only the fellow they take me for.

BUTLER

[*More astonished than ever*]
What do you say, Signore?

LAUDISI

You really think they're the same man?

BUTLER

[*As above, miserably attempting a smile, his mouth open*]
I don't understand.

LAUDISI

Who are you talking to?

BUTLER

[*Dumbfounded*]
What?! Who am I talking to? You, Signore!!!!

LAUDISI

And you're quite sure I'm the same man those ladies are asking for?

BUTLER

Well, Signore . . . I wouldn't know. . . . They said the mistress's brother . . .

LAUDISI

Oh, I see . . . in that case, it *is* me, isn't it? . . .
show them in, show them in . . .

[*The Butler withdraws but turns several times to
look at Laudisi. He hardly believes his own eyes.*]

Scene 4

THE SAME, SIGNORA CINI, SIGNORA NENNI

SIGNORA CINI

May we come in?

LAUDISI

Please do, Signora.

SIGNORA CINI

They told me Signora Agazzi isn't here. I have brought
my friend Signora Nenni with me. [*She introduces
Signora Nenni, an old woman even more foolish and
affected than herself. She too is full of greedy curiosity but is wary, upset.*] She *so* much wished to meet the
Signora—

LAUDISI

Signora Frola?

SIGNORA CINI

No, no, Signora Agazzi, your sister.

LAUDISI

Oh, she'll be coming, she'll be here soon. Signora Frola
too. Please be seated. [*He invites them to sit on the lit-*

tle sofa. Then deftly inserting himself between them]
May I? Three can sit on it quite comfortably. Signora
Sirelli is with them.

SIGNORA CINI

Yes. The butler told us.

LAUDISI

It's all arranged, you know. Oh, it'll be such a scene,
such a scene! Soon. At eleven o'clock. Here.

SIGNORA CINI

[*Dizzy*]
Arranged? What's arranged?

LAUDISI

[*Mysteriously, first with a gesture—that of joining
the tips of his forefingers—then with his voice*]
The meeting. [*A gesture of admiration*] A great idea!

SIGNORA CINI

What—what meeting?

LAUDISI

A meeting of those two. First, *he* will come in *here*.
[*He points towards the door on the left.*]

SIGNORA CINI

Signor Ponza?

LAUDISI

Yes. And *she* will be brought in *there*. [*He points
towards the music room.*]

SIGNORA CINI

Signora Frola?

Right You Are at Westport, Connecticut, 1952
directed by Eric Bentley

Mildred Dunnock as Signora Frola, Paula Laurence as Amalia

Dwight Marfield as Sirelli, Karl Redcoff as the Governor, Bert Freed
as Agazzi

Mildred Dunnock as Signora Frola, Alfred Drake as Laudisi, Martin Kosleck
as Ponza

Mildred Dunnock as Signora Frola, Alfred Drake as Laudisi, Florence
Sundstrom as Signora Sirelli, Queenie Smith as Signora Cini, Catharine
Doucet as Signora Nenni

LAUDISI

Precisely. [*Again, with an expressive gesture first, then with his voice*] Can't you see it? Both of them here on this sofa, the one confronting the other, and the rest of us all around watching and listening? A great idea!

SIGNORA CINI

In order to find out——

LAUDISI

The truth! But we know it already. Nothing remains but to unmask it.

SIGNORA CINI

[*With surprise and the keenest anxiety*] Ah! We know it already? Who is it then? Which of the two? Which is it?

LAUDISI

Let's see. Guess. Which would you say?

SIGNORA CINI

[*Hesitant*]
Well . . . I . . . look . . .

LAUDISI

He or she? Let's see . . . Guess . . . Come on!

SIGNORA CINI

I . . . I guess . . . him!

LAUDISI

[*Looks at her for a moment*]
He it is!

SIGNORA CINI

[*Tickled*]
It is? Ah, so that's it. Of course! It *had* to be him!

SIGNORA NENNI

[*Tickled*]
Him! We said so. We women said so.

SIGNORA CINI

And how did it come to light? Are there proofs? Documents?

SIGNORA NENNI

The police department found them, I suppose? We said so. With the Governor's authority behind us, we couldn't fail!

LAUDISI

[*Motions them to come closer, and then speaks quietly to them, mysteriously, weighing each syllable*]
The license of the second marriage!

SIGNORA CINI

[*Taking it like a blow on the nose*]
Second?

SIGNORA NENNI

[*Bewildered*]
What's that? The *second* marriage?

SIGNORA CINI

[*Reviving, but put out*]
Then . . . then *he* was right!

LAUDISI

Facts are facts, dear ladies. The license of the second
marriage—so it seems—is pretty clear.

SIGNORA NENNI

[*Almost weeping*]
Then *she* is the mad one!

LAUDISI

Yes, it does seem to be she.

SIGNORA CINI

What's this? Before, you said him, now you say her?

LAUDISI

Yes, dear lady, because the license—this license of the
second marriage—could quite well have been gotten
up with the help of friends to strengthen his delusion
that his present wife is his second. A forged document,
understand? In line with Signora Frola's explanation.

SIGNORA CINI

Ah! A document—without validity?

LAUDISI

That is, that is to say . . . with whatever validity,
dear ladies, with whatever value anyone wants to give
it. Remember, there are also the messages Signora
Frola says she received every day from her daughter.
Let down into the courtyard in a basket. There are those
messages, aren't there?

SIGNORA CINI

What if there are?

LAUDISI

More documents, Signora! Even these written messages are documents, with whatever value you wish to
give them. Signor Ponza comes along and says they're
forged—just done to strengthen Signora Frola's delusion.

SIGNORA CINI

Oh dear, then we know nothing for certain?

LAUDISI

Nothing, how do you mean, nothing? Let's not exaggerate. Tell me, how many days are there in the week?

SIGNORA CINI

Why, seven.

LAUDISI

Monday, Tuesday, Wednesday . . .

SIGNORA CINI

[*Feeling invited to continue*]
Thursday, Friday, Saturday—

LAUDISI

Sunday! [*Turning to the other woman*] And months in
the year?

SIGNORA NENNI

Twelve!

LAUDISI

January, February, March . . .

SIGNORA CINI

[*Struck with a bright idea*]
We've got it: you want to make fun of us!!

Scene 5

THE SAME, DINA

DINA

[*Suddenly comes running in*]
Uncle, please . . . [*Seeing Signora Cini, she stops.*]
Oh, Signora, you here?

SIGNORA CINI

Yes, I came with Signora Nenni—

LAUDISI

Who *so* much wanted to meet Signora Frola.

SIGNORA NENNI

No, no, please . . .

SIGNORA CINI

Go on teasing us! Oh, Dina dear, he's been getting us
all mixed up! I feel like a train entering a station:
poum, poum, poum, poum, all the time switching from
one track to another! We're dizzy!

DINA

Oh, he's being so naughty. With all of us. But wait. We
have all the proof we need now— I'll just tell Mother
you're here, and we'll drop the whole thing. Oh, Uncle,

if you only heard her! What a wonderful old lady she
is! How she talks! How good she is! Her apartment is
so neat, so elegant, everything in order, white covers
on the furniture . . . She showed us all her daughter's letters.

SIGNORA CINI

Very well . . . but if . . . as Signor Laudisi was
saying . . .

DINA

What does *he* know about it? He hasn't read them!

SIGNORA NENNI

Couldn't they be forged?

DINA

Forged, what *do* you mean? Could a mother mistake
her daughter's way of saying things? The last letter,
yesterday . . . [*She stops—hearing the sound of
voices from the music room.*] Ah, there they are, they
must be back already. [*She goes to the curtains to
look.*]

SIGNORA CINI

[*Following her at a run*]
With her? With Signora Frola?

DINA

Yes, you two come with me. We all have to be in the
music room. Is it eleven yet, Uncle?

Scene 6

THE SAME, AMALIA

AMALIA

[*Suddenly coming in from the music room. She too is agitated.*]
We can do without now: there's no further need of proof!

DINA

Quite right. Just what I think.

AMALIA

[*Hastily acknowledging Signora Cini's presence, sad and anxious*]
How are you, Signora?

SIGNORA CINI

[*Introducing Signora Nenni*]
This is Signora Nenni. She came with me to—

AMALIA

[*Hurriedly greeting Signora Nenni too*]
A pleasure, I'm sure. [*Pause*] There's no further doubt. It's *he!*

SIGNORA CINI

It's *he?* You're sure it's *he?*

DINA

Let's not go on deceiving the old lady this way, let's tell Father it's all off.

AMALIA

Oh, this bringing her over to our apartment, it's a betrayal!

LAUDISI

Oh, an outrage, an outrage, you're right! It's even becoming clear to me that she's the one. She must be, she *is!*

AMALIA

She's the one? What? What do you say?

LAUDISI

I say it's she, she, she!

AMALIA

Oh, stop it!

DINA

We're quite sure the opposite is the case!

SIGNORA CINI AND SIGNORA NENNI

[*Overjoyed, to Laudisi*]
Really? You really mean it's she?

LAUDISI

Sure, I mean it. You're all very certain—and *I'm* all very certain!

DINA

Oh, come on, let's get out of here. Don't you see he's doing it on purpose?

AMALIA

Yes. Let's get out, ladies. [*In the doorway*] Please excuse us.

[*Exeunt Signora Cini, Signora Nenni, Amalia. Dina starts to go.*]

LAUDISI

[*Calling her to him*]
Dina!

DINA

I don't want to listen to you. Leave me alone.

LAUDISI

Let's close these doors—if there's no further need of proof.

DINA

What about Father? It's he that's left them open. He'll be here any moment with that man. If he found them closed . . . You know Father.

LAUDISI

But you'd all explain—*you* would, especially—that there was no need to keep them open. Aren't you convinced?

DINA

Utterly.

LAUDISI

[*With a challenging smile*]
Then close them.

DINA

You want the pleasure of seeing I still haven't decided.
I won't close the doors—but only because of Father.

LAUDISI

[*As above*]
Shall *I* close them then?

DINA

That's entirely your affair.

LAUDISI

Unlike you, I can't claim to be sure it's he that's mad.

DINA

Just come into the music room and listen to the old lady
for a minute as we have. You'll not have a doubt in the
world. Will you come?

LAUDISI

Yes, I'll come. And I can close the doors? Since it's entirely my affair?

DINA

I see. Even before you hear her talk . . .

LAUDISI

No, my dear. It's because I'm sure that by this time your
father agrees that there's no need of proof.

DINA

Father agrees?

LAUDISI

Of course. He's talking with *him*. There can, therefore, be no doubt: by this time he's certain it's *she* that's mad. [*He approaches the folding doors with decision.*] I'll close the doors.

DINA

[*Suddenly restraining him*]
No. [*Then, correcting herself*] I'm sorry . . . but if that's what you think . . . we'd better leave them open . . . [*Laudisi bursts into his usual laugh.*] I mean because of Father.

LAUDISI

Your father will say because of the rest of you. But we can leave them open.
[*From the music room comes the sound of the piano. It is an old melody, full of sweet and mournful grace, "Il mio ben, quando verrà?" from the opera* Nina Mad Through Love *by Paisiello.*]

DINA

Ah! It's she, do you hear? It's *she*, playing!

LAUDISI

The old lady?

DINA

Yes. She told us her daughter was always playing that tune. In the old days. Do you hear how sweetly she plays? Let's go in.

Scene 7

AGAZZI, PONZA, *then* SIRELLI

After Laudisi and Dina have left, the stage is empty for a while. The sound of the piano from the next room continues. Then Ponza comes in by the door on the left with Agazzi. Hearing the music, he is profoundly disturbed; he becomes more and more so, as the present scene progresses.

AGAZZI

[In the doorway]
After you, after you, please. [*He has Ponza enter, then he himself enters, and goes towards the desk to take the papers that he has pretended to forget.*] Here's where I must have left them. Please be seated. [*Ponza remains standing. He looks agitatedly towards the music room whence the sound of the music is still pouring.*] And here they are, in fact! [*He takes the papers and approaches Ponza, leafing through them.*] It's a suit that's been dragging on for years, as I was telling you, a mess of complications! [*He too turns towards the music room, irritated by the piano.*] This music! At such a moment! [*Turning he makes a gesture of contempt, as if to say: "These women!"*] Who is playing? [*He goes to look into the music room through the open door, sees Signora Frola at the piano. Gesture of amazement*] Ah! Look!!

PONZA

[Coming over to him, convulsed]
In God's name, is it she? Is *she* playing?

AGAZZI

Yes. It's your mother-in-law! How well she plays!

PONZA

But what *is* this? They've brought her here—again? And they make her play?

AGAZZI

Well, I don't see any harm in that.

PONZA

But, please, not *that*, not *that* tune! It's the one her daughter used to play.

AGAZZI

Oh dear, it hurts you to hear her play it?

PONZA

It's not me. It hurts *her*. It does her incalculable harm. I told you, Councillor, I told the ladies what the condition of poor Signora Frola is—

AGAZZI

[*Endeavoring to calm him in his ever increasing agitation*]
Yes, yes . . . but . . .

PONZA

[*Continuing*]
And that she must be left in peace! That she can't receive visits—or pay them! I'm the only one—the only one—who knows how to look after her. You are ruining her, ruining her!

AGAZZI

Not at all. How so? Our women folk know perfectly
well . . .

[*The music suddenly stops, and so does Agazzi. A
chorus of approval is heard from the music room.*]
You see? . . . Just listen . . .

[*From the music room the two following speeches
are heard:*]

DINA

You still play wonderfully, Signora!

SIGNORA FROLA

I play wonderfully? What about Lina? You should
hear my daughter Lina. How *she* plays!

PONZA

[*Fretting, digging his nails into his hands*]
Do you hear?! She say, "my daughter Lina"?!

AGAZZI

Yes, of course, her daughter.
[*Again from the music room:*]

SIGNORA FROLA

No, it's true, she's not been able to play. Since that
time. That's maybe what gives her most pain, poor
child!

AGAZZI

It seems natural enough . . . she thinks her still
alive . . .

PONZA

But you mustn't make her say these things. She mustn't say them. Did you hear? "Since that time." She said "since that time." Because it's the old piano. You don't know. It's the piano my first wife played.

[*At this point Sirelli comes in by the door on the left. When he hears Ponza's last words and notes his extreme exasperation, he stops in his tracks, dumbfounded. Agazzi is also dismayed but signals to him to come over.*]

AGAZZI

Ask the ladies to come in here, will you?

[*Giving the two men a wide berth, Sirelli goes to the music room and calls the ladies.*]

PONZA

The ladies? Here?! No, no! Better . . .

Scene 8

THE SAME, SIGNORA FROLA, SIGNORA AMALIA
SIGNORA SIRELLI, DINA, SIGNORA CINI
SIGNORA NENNI, LAUDISI

Having seen Sirelli's dismay, the ladies and Laudisi are quite upset as they come in. Signora Frola, seeing her son-in-law's extreme excitement—he is shaking all over, like an animal in pain—is panic-stricken. When he rails against her in the following scene with the utmost violence, from time to time she gives the company significant looks. The scene is swift and tense.

PONZA

You—here? Here—again? What have you come for?

SIGNORA FROLA

Well, I came . . . don't be impatient . . .

PONZA

You came here to repeat . . . What have you been saying, what have you been saying to these ladies?

SIGNORA FROLA

Nothing, I swear, nothing!

PONZA

Nothing? What do you mean, nothing? I heard! This gentleman heard too! [*He points at Agazzi.*] You said "she plays." *Who* plays? Lina? You know perfectly well your daughter has been dead for four years.

SIGNORA FROLA

Of course she has, my dear. Please be calm!

PONZA

You said "she hasn't been able to play any more—since that time." How right you are: she hasn't been able to play since that time—because she's *dead!*

SIGNORA FROLA

Yes, yes, quite. Didn't I say so myself, ladies? Didn't I say she hasn't been able to play since that time? She's dead!

PONZA

Then why do you still think about the piano?

Right You Are, as produced by the Theatre Guild, New York, 1927
directed by Philip Moeller

Henry Travers as Sirelli, Morris Carnovsky as Agazzi, Beryl Mercer as
Signora Frola, Laura Hope Crews as Amalia, Elisabeth Risdon as Signora
Sirelli, Phyllis Connard as Dina, Helen Westley as Signora Cini, Reginald
Mason as Laudisi

Dorothy Fletcher as Signora
Nenni, Helen Westley as
Signora Cini, Reginald Mason
as Laudisi

Right You Are, as produced by the Theatre Guild, New York, 1927 directed by Philip Moeller

Edward G. Robinson as Ponza, Armina Marshall as Signora Ponza, Beryl Mercer as Signora Frola

Photo by Florence Vandamm

Edward G. Robinson as Ponza, Beryl Mercer as Signora Frola

Photo by Florence Vandamm

SIGNORA FROLA

I don't, I honestly don't, I never think of it!

PONZA

I smashed it. As you well know. I smashed it when your daughter died. So that this—other—wife couldn't touch it—and in any case she can't play! You know she doesn't play!

SIGNORA FROLA

Certainly she can't play, certainly!

PONZA

And what was her name? She was called Lina, wasn't she—your daughter? Now tell these people what my second wife is called. Just tell them. You know well enough: what's her name?

SIGNORA FROLA

Julia. Her name is Julia. But it *is*, I tell you: it's Julia!

PONZA

Julia, then. Not Lina. And this winking at people— when you tell them her name's Julia—don't do it!

SIGNORA FROLA

Winking? I wasn't winking!

PONZA

Yes, you were, I saw you, you were winking at them all, you want to ruin me, you want these people to believe I still wish to keep your daughter all to myself as if she weren't dead at all. [*He breaks down in terrible sobs.*] As if she weren't dead at all!

SIGNORA FROLA

[*Quickly, with infinite tenderness and humility, running to him*]
I want that? No, *no*, NO, dearest! Please be calm now. I never said such things—did I, did I, ladies?

AMALIA AND SIGNORA SIRELLI

No, no, she never said anything of the sort. She always said she was dead!

SIGNORA FROLA

Yes, didn't I? I said she's dead. Of course. And that you're so kind to me. [*To the ladies*] I did, didn't I? Ruin you? Hurt you? I?

PONZA

[*Rising, terrible*]
All the same you go around in other people's houses looking for a piano. Then you play the sonatinas she used to play—and tell them "Lina plays them like this, Lina plays them better!"

SIGNORA FROLA

No, it was . . . just . . . to show . . .

PONZA

But you can't! You mustn't! Playing the pieces your dead daughter used to play—how can you possibly think of such a thing?

SIGNORA FROLA

You're right, poor boy—poor boy! [*She is deeply touched and weeps.*] I'll never do it again, never, never again!

PONZA

[*Coming close to her, with terrible violence*]
Go! Get out! Get out!

SIGNORA FROLA

Yes, yes . . . I'm going, I'm going . . . Oh, dear! [*Backing out, she sends beseeching looks to the company, as if asking that they be considerate to her son-in-law. Weeping, she withdraws.*]

Scene 9

THE SAME, *minus* SIGNORA FROLA

Overcome with pity and terror, they look at Ponza. But he, as soon as his mother-in-law has left, completely changes his mood. He is calm. He re-assumes his normal manner, and says simply

PONZA

I must ask you all to forgive me for the scene I had to make. It was a necessary remedy for the harm you had done her, with your compassion. Of course you didn't intend it. You didn't even know.

AGAZZI

[*Astounded, like all the others*]
What? You were just pretending?

PONZA

I had to, I'm afraid. It's the only way, don't you see,
to hold her to her illusion—my shouting out the truth
like that—as if it were madness? You will forgive me,
won't you? And I must beg to be excused; *she* needs
me. [*He leaves, hurriedly. Once more they are all
astounded, silent, looking each other over.*]

LAUDISI

[*Coming center*]
So this, my friends, is the truth! [*He bursts out laughing.*]

Act III~Scene 1

LAUDISI *is lounging in an armchair, reading. Through the folding doors that lead to the music room comes the confused noise of many voices. The* BUTLER *brings in* POLICE COMMISSIONER CENTURI *through the door on the left.*

BUTLER

Will you come in here, please? I'll go and tell the Councillor.

LAUDISI

[*Turns and notices Centuri*]
Oh, Commissioner Centuri!
[*He rises hurriedly and recalls the Butler.*] Wait a moment!
[*To Centuri*] Any news?

CENTURI

[*Tall, stiff, frowning, about forty*]
Well yes, we *have* heard something.

LAUDISI

Oh, good.
[*To the Butler*] You may go. I'll call my brother-in-law myself, when the time comes. [*He indicates the folding doors with a nod. The Butler bows and goes out.*]
So you've performed the miracle. You're saving a city. You hear? You hear the noise they're making? Well, is the news definite?

CENTURI

We *have* managed to track down a few people—

LAUDISI

From Ponza's village? They know about him?

CENTURI

Yes—up to a point. The few facts we have seem certain.

LAUDISI

Oh, good, good. What, for example?

CENTURI

Well, here are the papers I've been sent. [*He takes an open yellow envelope with a document in it out of the inside pocket of his coat and hands it to Laudisi.*]

LAUDISI

Let's see, let's see. [*He takes the document out of the envelope and reads it to himself, from time to time interjecting an oh! or an ah!—his tone changing from satisfaction to doubt, then to something like commiseration, and finally to complete disenchantment.*] No, no, no! This amounts to absolutely nothing, there's nothing definite in this, Commissioner.

CENTURI

That's all we could find out.

LAUDISI

But not one of the doubtful points is cleared up. [*Looks at him, then with sudden resolution*] Do you want to

do a good deed, Commissioner? Perform a distin-
guished service to the community and earn the gratitude of God Almighty?

CENTURI

[*Looking at him, perplexed*]
What service do you mean, exactly?

LAUDISI

Well, look. Sit down there. [*He points to the desk.*]
Tear up this half-page of information, it doesn't get
us any further. And on the other half of the page write
something precise and certain.

CENTURI

[*Astonished*]
Me? What do you mean? What sort of thing?

LAUDISI

Anything. Whatever you like. In the name of his two
fellow townsmen, the ones you tracked down. For the
general good! To restore peace and quiet to our town!
They want something *true*—it doesn't matter *what*—so
long as it's good and factual, categorical, specific. You
give it to them!

CENTURI

[*With emphasis, getting heated, and more or less
offended*]
How can I give it to them if I don't have it? Do you wish
me to commit forgery? I'm amazed you dare propose
such a thing to me. I'm more than amazed, in fact. Now
that's enough: please present me to Councillor Agazzi
at once!

LAUDISI

[*Opens his arms in a gesture of surrender*]
At once.

[*He goes over to the folding doors and opens them.
Immediately the noise of all the people in the music
room is louder. But as soon as Laudisi steps through
the doorway the shouting stops. From the music room
one hears Laudisi's voice announcing: "Commissioner
Centuri has arrived. He has definite news from people
who know!" Applause and cries of hooray greet the
announcement. Commissioner Centuri gets disturbed
because he knows the information he brings will not
suffice to satisfy so much expectation.*]

Scene 2

THE SAME, AGAZZI, SIRELLI, LAUDISI, AMALIA, DINA
SIGNORA SIRELLI, SIGNORA CINI, SIGNORA NENNI
AND MANY OTHER MEN AND WOMEN

They all rush in with AGAZZI *at their head, inflamed,
exultant, clapping their hands and shouting.*

ALL

Good work, Centuri!

AGAZZI

[*With arms outstretched*]
My dear Centuri, I was sure of it: you couldn't miss!

ALL

Good work, good work! Let's see, let's see the proofs!
Right now! Who is it? Which is the one?

CENTURI

[*Astonished, uncomprehending, lost*]
There's some mistake . . . I er . . . well, Councillor . . .

AGAZZI

Please, ladies and gentlemen, quiet, please!

CENTURI

It's true, I . . . er, left no stone unturned, but if Signor Laudisi says I also—

AGAZZI

That you also bring definite news!

SIRELLI

Precise facts!

LAUDISI

[*Loudly, decisively, warningly*]
Not many facts but precise ones! From people he man-
aged to track down. In Signor Ponza's own village.
People who know.

ALL

At last! Oh, at last, at last!

CENTURI

[*Shrugging, presenting the document to Agazzi*]
Here you are, Councillor.

AGAZZI

[*Opening it up amid the press of all the people who are milling around*]
Now let's see, let's see.

CENTURI

[*Resentful, approaching Laudisi*]
Now really, Signor Laudisi . . .

LAUDISI

[*Quickly, loudly*]
Let him read it, for heaven's sake, let him read it!

AGAZZI

Just be patient one moment longer, ladies and gentlemen. And don't press so close, I can't read! *That's* better.

[*There is a moment's pause. Then, into the silence, is projected the precise, firm voice of Laudisi.*]

LAUDISI

I've already read it!

ALL

[*Leaving Agazzi and rushing noisily over to Laudisi*]
You have? Well? What does it say? They know the answer?

LAUDISI

[*Very formally*]
It is certain, it is irrefutable, we have the testimony of a fellow townsman of Signor Ponza's—that Signora Frola has been in a sanitarium!

ALL

[*Disappointed, crestfallen*]
Oh!

SIGNORA SIRELLI

Signora Frola?

DINA

Was it definitely she?

AGAZZI

[*Who has read the document in the meantime, waves it, and shouts*]
No, no, no! There's nothing of the sort here at all!

ALL

[*Leaving Laudisi, they rush back to Agazzi, shouting*]
What's this? What do you say, what do you say?

LAUDISI

[*Loudly, to Agazzi*]
But there is! It says "the lady." It specifically says "the lady"!

AGAZZI

[*Louder*]
Not at all! This man only says he "thinks" so, he isn't even sure. In any event he doesn't profess to know if it was mother or daughter!

ALL

[*Satisfied*]
Ah!

LAUDISI

[*Insisting*]
But it must be the mother, it must be!

SIRELLI

Not in the least, it's the daughter, it's the daughter!

SIGNORA SIRELLI

Besides the old lady told us so herself!

AMALIA

Exactly—that's right—when they took the poor girl
from her husband secretly—

DINA

—and shut her up in a sanitarium!

AGAZZI

Besides, this informant isn't even from the same village. He says he "often went there," that he "doesn't
quite recall," that "he thinks he heard it said" . . .

SIRELLI

Oh, just hearsay!

LAUDISI

Excuse me for saying so, but if you're all so convinced
that Signora Frola is right, what more do you want?
Have done with the whole thing once and for all! It's he
that's mad, and that's all there is to say.

SIRELLI

That's all very well, my dear man, if we could ignore
the Governor's opinion. But he believes just the oppo-

site. He makes a great show of the confidence he feels
in Signor Ponza and *his* version of the story.

CENTURI

That's very true. The Governor believes in Signor
Ponza, he told *me* so too!

AGAZZI

But this is because the Governor hasn't talked with the
old lady next door.

SIGNORA SIRELLI

Exactly! He's only talked with *him!*

SIRELLI

But there are others who agree with the Governor!

A MAN

I do, for instance! I do! Because I know a similar case:
a mother who's gone mad at the death of her daughter
and believes her son-in-law is refusing to let her see the
girl. The same thing!

SECOND MAN

Oh no, because *that* son-in-law has remained a widower
and lives alone, whereas Signor Ponza is not alone,
he—

LAUDISI

[*As an idea dawns on him*]
Good heavens, do you hear that? Now we have the
answer. For heaven's sake—Columbus's egg! [*Clapping the Second Man on the shoulder*] Good work, my
dear fellow! Did you all hear what he said?

ALL

[*Perplexed, not comprehending*]
What's this? *What* did he say?

SECOND MAN

[*Amazed*]
What did I say? I've no idea . . .

LAUDISI

What did he say? But he's solved the whole question.
Hold on a minute, everybody! [*To Agazzi*] The Governor is to come here?

AGAZZI

Yes, we're expecting him . . . But why? Explain.

LAUDISI

It's no use his coming here to talk with Signora Frola.
Up to now he believes in her son-in-law. When he's
talked with the old lady he won't know himself which
of the two to believe. No, that won't do. It's something
else that the Governor must do here. One thing in particular.

ALL

And what's that?

LAUDISI

[*With an air of triumph*]
What is it? Didn't you hear what our friend said? "Signor Ponza is not alone." In other words, he has a wife!

SIRELLI

You mean, we could get his *wife* to talk?! I see, I see.

DINA

But he keeps her locked up, doesn't he?

SIRELLI

The Governor would have to use his authority and *order* her to speak!

AMALIA

Certainly, she's the one to tell us the truth!

SIGNORA SIRELLI

How so? She'd say whatever her husband wants.

LAUDISI

Yes—*if* she had to talk with him present.

SIRELLI

Then she should talk with the Governor in private!

AGAZZI

Surely. The authority of the Governor will do the trick. When she's alone with him she'll undoubtedly explain just how things really are, of course she will, don't you agree, Centuri?

CENTURI

Not a doubt of it—if the Governor is interested!

AGAZZI

It's the only way. We must tell him about it and spare him the trouble of coming over. Would you mind looking after it, Centuri?

CENTURI

Not a bit. I'll go at once. Good day, everyone. [*He bows and leaves.*]

SIGNORA SIRELLI

[*Clapping her hands*]
At last! Good for Laudisi!

DINA

Good old uncle, what a clever idea!

ALL

Good work, good work! Yes, it's the only way, the only way!

AGAZZI

Of course. Why didn't we think of it before?

SIRELLI

Think of it. No one's ever seen her. It's as if the poor woman didn't exist!

LAUDISI

[*Struck with another bright idea*]
Oh! By the way, you're all sure she exists?

AMALIA

Now really, Lamberto!

SIRELLI

[*Pretending to laugh*]
You want us to doubt her very existence?

LAUDISI

Just a minute. You say yourselves no one has ever seen her!

DINA

Not at all. There's the old lady who sees her and talks to her every day.

SIGNORA SIRELLI

What's more, her husband admits it.

LAUDISI

Very good. But reflect a moment. To be strictly logical, all you'd expect to find in that apartment is a phantom. A ghost.

ALL

A ghost?

AGAZZI

Oh come on, drop it for once.

LAUDISI

Let me finish. The ghost of a second wife, if Signora Frola is right. The ghost of her daughter, if Signor Ponza is right. It remains to be seen, my friends, if what is a ghost to husband or mother, is also a real person—to herself. Having come so far, we can permit ourselves to doubt it.

AMALIA

Run along with you. You just want everyone to be as mad as you.

SIGNORA NENNI

Good heavens, it gives me the creeps!

SIGNORA CINI

I don't know what pleasure it can give you to frighten us this way!

ALL

Nothing of the sort! He's joking!

SIRELLI

She's a woman of flesh and blood, there's no reason to doubt it. And we'll get her to talk, we'll get her to talk!

AGAZZI

It was you yourself that proposed to have her talk with the Governor—just a minute ago!

LAUDISI

Why, yes, if it's really a woman that's up in that apartment—a woman in the ordinary sense of the word. But think it over, ladies and gentlemen, how *can* it be a woman in the ordinary sense of the word? It can't. That's why I say I doubt her very existence.

SIGNORA SIRELLI

Heavens, he *is* trying to drive us mad!

LAUDISI

Well, we'll see, we'll see.

ALL

[*Confused voices*]
But other people have seen her, haven't they? She

comes out in the courtyard, doesn't she? She writes
messages to her mother. He's doing this just to make
fun of us!

Scene 3

THE SAME, CENTURI

CENTURI

[*Entering amid the general hubbub, excited, and
announcing*]
The Governor is here! The Governor is here!

AGAZZI

The Governor here? What have you been up to?

CENTURI

I met him on his way over—with Signor Ponza—

SIRELLI

With Signor Ponza!

AGAZZI

Heavens, no! If he's with Ponza, they're probably going to visit the old lady next door. Please, Centuri,
will you wait outside and ask the Governor to step in
here for a moment as he promised me?

CENTURI

Certainly, sir. [*He leaves in haste through the door on
the left.*]

AGAZZI

My friends, I must ask you to retire to the music room for a while.

SIGNORA SIRELLI

You'll put it to him properly, won't you? It's the only way, the only way!

AMALIA

This way, ladies, please!

AGAZZI

You'll stay, won't you, Sirelli? You too, Lamberto. [*The others all go into the music room. To Laudisi*] But let me do the talking, won't you?

LAUDISI

I'll be glad to. In fact if you'd prefer me to leave too . . .

AGAZZI

Oh no, it's better if you stay. [*He closes the folding doors.*] Ah, here he comes.

Scene 4

LAUDISI, AGAZZI, SIRELLI, THE GOVERNOR, CENTURI

GOVERNOR

[*About sixty, tall, fat, an air of complaisant good nature. Entering by door on left*]
My dear Agazzi! Oh, you're here, are you, Sirelli? My dear Laudisi! [*He shakes hands all round.*]

LAUDISI

How are you, Governor?

AGAZZI

Come right in, Centuri, sit here, will you? Sirelli, you sit there. Will you sit here, Governor? I hope you don't mind my asking you to come here first?

GOVERNOR

I was intending to come, just as I promised. I'd have come afterwards anyway. Well, Sirelli, I've been hearing about you. They tell me you're all inflamed and agitated over this matter of the new secretary—more agitated than anyone else!

SIRELLI

That's not quite true, Governor. I don't think you can find anyone in town who's not just as agitated as I am.

AGAZZI

That is so. Everybody's terribly agitated.

GOVERNOR

Well, I can't for the life of me understand why.

AGAZZI

Because it hasn't been your lot to see certain goings on. Now *we* have the old lady right next door, his mother-in-law, you know—

SIRELLI

Forgive me, Governor, but you haven't heard what she has to say, have you?

GOVERNOR

I was just going to see her. [*To Agazzi*] I'd promised
you I'd listen to her here as you wished. But her son-in-
law came to beg me to go to her place. He was desperate about it—it's all the gossip that bothers him. Now
the point is, do you think he'd send me to her if he
weren't quite sure the visit would confirm his own version of the story?

AGAZZI

Certainly he would. When *he's* present, the old lady—

SIRELLI

[*Cutting in*]
Would say whatever he wants her to say, Governor!
And that's the proof that it's not she that's mad!

AGAZZI

We put it to the test, right here, only yesterday!

GOVERNOR

Well, yes, but he deliberately makes her believe it's
he that's mad. He forewarned me of that. How otherwise could the poor old thing keep her illusion? But
think what torture it is for poor Ponza!

SIRELLI

That is, if it's not *she* who permits *him* the illusion of
believing her daughter dead—so he won't live in con-
stant fear of her being taken away again! In that case,
you must realize, Governor, it's the old lady who's
being tortured now, not Ponza.

AGAZZI

Well, that's the point at issue. I'm sure *you*— [*To the Governor*] must be wondering—

SIRELLI

We're *all* wondering—

GOVERNOR

But are you? Not very seriously, I think. None of you seem to have any doubts about the matter. I'm on the other side, and I have no doubts either. What about you, Laudisi?

LAUDISI

Pardon me, Governor; I've promised my brother-in-law to hold my tongue.

AGAZZI

[*With a start*]
Now really, what are you saying? If you're asked a question, reply for heaven's sake! You know why I asked him to be quiet, don't you? Because for the past two days he's been amusing himself making the mystery more mysterious.

LAUDISI

Don't believe him, Governor. It's just the other way round: I've been doing my best to clear the mystery up.

SIRELLI

Oh yes, and d'you know how? By maintaining it's impossible to discover the truth. By creating the suspi-

cion that there's no woman in Ponza's house at all—
but a ghost!

GOVERNOR

[*Enjoying it all*]
What, really? Not so bad!

AGAZZI

Oh, please! You know *him;* it's no use taking any notice of *him.*

LAUDISI

Though it was through me you were invited over, Governor.

GOVERNOR

Because you also think I'd do well to talk with the old
lady next door?

LAUDISI

Nothing of the kind. You do best to stick by Signor
Ponza's version of the story.

GOVERNOR

Oh, I see. So you agree that Signor Ponza—

LAUDISI

[*Quickly*]
No! I want all the others to stick by Signora Frola's
version and make an end of the matter.

AGAZZI

You see how it is? Would you call that logic?

GOVERNOR

One moment.

[*To Laudisi*] In your opinion, then, what the old lady says is also trustworthy?

LAUDISI

Absolutely. From beginning to end. Like what *he* says.

GOVERNOR

What are we to make of it then—

SIRELLI

If what they say is contradictory?

AGAZZI

[*Irritated, with decision*]
Would you listen to me for a moment? I haven't committed myself. I lean to neither one version nor the other—and I don't intend to till later. *He* may be right, *she* may be right. The point is we must find out. And there's but one way to do so.

SIRELLI

And— [*Pointing at Laudisi*] he has suggested what it is.

GOVERNOR

He has? Well, let's hear it.

AGAZZI

Since none of the other evidence amounts to proof, the only thing is for you to use your authority and extract a confession from the wife!

GOVERNOR

Signora Ponza?

SIRELLI

Not in the presence of her husband, naturally.

AGAZZI

In private. So she'll tell the truth.

SIRELLI

So she'll explain whether she's the old lady's daughter
as we think she must be—

AGAZZI

Or whether she's a second wife who's agreed to play the
part of the old lady's daughter as Signor Ponza would
have us believe—

GOVERNOR

And as I certainly believe myself! Well, by all means.
This seems the only way to me too. Poor Ponza himself desires nothing better than to convince everyone
he is right. He's been utterly accommodating. He'll be
happier than anybody about this. And it will certainly
ease *your* minds, my friends. Will you do something
for me, Centuri?
    [*Centuri rises.*]
Go and bring Signor Ponza from next door. Tell him
I'd like to see him a moment.

CENTURI

Certainly. [*Bows and leaves*]

AGAZZI

If only he consents!

GOVERNOR

He'll consent at once, just watch! We'll make an end of the whole matter in the space of a few minutes. Right here before your eyes.

AGAZZI

What? In *my* place?

SIRELLI

You think he'll want to bring his wife *here?*

GOVERNOR

Leave me alone. I said: right here. Because otherwise you'll all be thinking *I*—

AGAZZI

No, no, no! What are you saying?

SIRELLI

That? Never!

GOVERNOR

Come off it. Since you know I felt sure all along that *he* was in the right, you'd think I was just hushing the matter up, protecting a public servant. No, I say! I want you all to hear. [*Then to Agazzi*] Is your wife at home?

AGAZZI

Yes, she's in the next room, with some other ladies . . .

GOVERNOR

Aha! Subversive activities in the back room! You can
hardly object if I make the place serve a more useful
purpose. Let's set the stage. We'll put Ponza here. Will
you and Sirelli sit opposite with me, Agazzi? That's it!

Scene 5

THE SAME, CENTURI, PONZA
CENTURI

Signor Ponza!

GOVERNOR

Thank you, Centuri. Please bring him in.
    [*Ponza appears in the doorway.*]

CENTURI

Come in, come right in, Signor Ponza.
    [*Ponza bows.*]

GOVERNOR

Please be seated, my dear Ponza.
    [*Ponza bows again and sits down.*]

GOVERNOR

You know these gentlemen . . . Sirelli . . .
    [*Ponza rises and bows.*]

AGAZZI

Yes, I already introduced them. That is Laudisi, my
brother-in-law.
    [*Ponza bows.*]

GOVERNOR

I sent for you, my dear Ponza, to tell you that here, with my friends . . .

[*No sooner has he started speaking than Ponza is visibly very disturbed, deeply agitated. The Governor, aware of this, stops.*]
You wish to say something?

PONZA

Yes. I ask to be transferred to another town. As of today.

GOVERNOR

But why? You spoke so reasonably with me not long ago, so . . .

PONZA

Yes, but now I'm the target of insufferable persecution.

GOVERNOR

Now, come: let's not exaggerate!

AGAZZI

[*To Ponza*]
Persecution, did you say? Do you mean by me?

PONZA

Persecution by everybody. And that's why I'm going. I'm going, Governor. A relentless, ferocious investigation of my private life—that's what it is—and I won't stand for it. It will end in ruining the . . . labor of love that I'm devoting my life to—not counting the cost. I love and respect that poor old lady more than if

she were my own mother; yet, yesterday, I was compelled to attack her with the most cruel violence. And
now, in her apartment, I find her in such a state of deg-
radation and over-excitement—

AGAZZI

[*Interrupting, calm*]
It's strange—because, to us, the old lady always spoke
with the utmost calm. The over-excitement was all
yours, Signor Ponza. And is so now!

PONZA

Because none of you know what you are making me go
through!

GOVERNOR

Come, come, calm yourself, my dear Ponza! What is
the matter? I am here. And you know with how much
trust and sympathy I've always listened to you, isn't
that true?

PONZA

It's true—as far as you're concerned. And I'm grateful, Governor.

GOVERNOR

Well then! Look, you love and respect your wife's
mother as if she were your own. I'd like you to realize
that my friends here are curious to find out the truth
precisely because *they* are fond of the old lady too.

PONZA

But they are killing her, Governor. I warned them re-
peatedly.

GOVERNOR

Really, my dear Ponza, once this thing is cleared up, you'll not be troubled by them again. And we'll clear it up right away, there's no problem. You yourself can remove the last doubt from the minds of these friends —not from mine, I'm already convinced—in the simplest, surest way.

PONZA

How so, if they don't believe a word I speak?

AGAZZI

That is not true. When you came here, after your mother-in-law's first visit, to tell us she was mad, we all believed you. We were amazed but we believed you. [*To the Governor*] But immediately afterwards, you understand, the old lady returned—

GOVERNOR

Yes, yes, I know, you told me . . . [*Continues, turning towards Ponza*] She returned to give the version of the story which you yourself wish her to accept. It's surely not so hard to see that a painful doubt might arise in the mind of anyone who heard *her* after hearing *you*. What it boils down to is that our friends have had difficulty in completely believing you, my dear Ponza, since they heard what your mother-in-law had to say. There's only one thing to do. You and your mother-in-law must retire for a moment. *You* feel sure you are telling the truth, *I* feel sure you are too. So you can't have anything against having it *re*-told by the only person—besides the two of you—that's in a position to re-tell it.

PONZA

Who is that?

GOVERNOR

Why—your wife?

PONZA

My wife? [*With force and indignation*] Oh, no!
Never!

GOVERNOR

And why not, may I ask?

PONZA

I'm to bring my wife here for the satisfaction of people
who won't believe me?

GOVERNOR

[*Promptly*]
I beg your pardon, it's for *my* satisfaction. Is it really
so hard to arrange?

PONZA

But, Governor! Not my wife! Don't ask that! Leave
my wife out of this! Just believe *me!*

GOVERNOR

Now, really, if you talk this way, I too will start thinking you don't *want* us to believe you.

AGAZZI

He tried in every possible way to stop his mother-in-
law coming here in the first place. Even at the cost of
being rude to my wife and daughter.

PONZA

[*Bursting out in sheer exasperation*]
What do you all want of me, in God's name? You've
had the old lady, wasn't that enough? Must you get
your hands on my wife too? I cannot put up with this
violence, Governor. My wife is not leaving our apartment! I won't hand her over. It's enough that *you* believe me. I'm filling out the blanks for my transfer.
Then I go. [*He rises.*]

GOVERNOR

[*Bringing down his fist on the desk*]
Wait! In the first place you will not speak in that tone
before Councillor Agazzi and me. I won't stand for it.
I have shown *you* courtesy and deference. In the second
place you are refusing to supply a proof which I—
and not the others—am asking for. I am asking for it
in *your* interest, I can't see how it can possibly harm
you. I repeat: your obstinacy makes *me* begin to doubt
you too. My colleague and I can perfectly well receive a lady—or even, if you prefer, come to your
home . . .

PONZA

You make it a matter of duty?

GOVERNOR

I repeat: I am *asking* this for your own good. My position entitles me to *demand* it.

PONZA

Very well, very well. If that's how it is. I will bring my
wife here, and have done with it. But who can guaran-
tee that the old lady won't see her?

GOVERNOR

Yes . . . it's true she's just next door . . .

AGAZZI

[*Quickly*]
*W*e could go to the Signora's apartment.

PONZA

No, no, it was you I was thinking of. I meant I don't want you to prepare any more of these catastrophic surprises.

AGAZZI

You needn't worry, as far as we're concerned.

GOVERNOR

Or, look, if it suits you better, you could take the lady to the Government Building.

PONZA

No, no, I'll bring her here at once. Then I'll go next door and keep an eye on Signora Frola. I'm going, Governor. Then it will be over, over! [*He leaves angrily.*]

Scene 6

THE SAME, *minus* PONZA

GOVERNOR

I didn't expect this opposition on his part, I must confess.

AGAZZI

Now he'll go and make his wife say what *he* wants said, just watch.

GOVERNOR

No, no. Don't worry about that. I shall question the lady myself.

SIRELLI

Really, the way he's always so worked up!

GOVERNOR

No, no, it's the first time—the very first—that I've seen him this way. Perhaps it's the idea of bringing his wife—

SIRELLI

The idea of setting her free, you mean!

GOVERNOR

Oh, his keeping her locked up—after all, that can be explained without assuming he's mad!

SIRELLI

Excuse me, Governor, you still haven't heard the old lady, poor creature!

AGAZZI

He says himself he keeps his wife locked up because of her mother.

GOVERNOR

Even if that isn't the case, he might still keep her locked up. He might be jealous. He might simply be a jealous husband.

SIRELLI

To the extent of not having a maid or a cleaning
woman? He compels his wife to do all the housework
herself.

AGAZZI

And *he* does the shopping. Every morning.

CENTURI

That's true, sir. I've seen him. He carries his parcels
home with a little boy to help him—

SIRELLI

—and the little boy stays outside!

GOVERNOR

But good heavens, he told me about that and sincerely
deplored it!

LAUDISI

[*Playfully*]
Reliable sources of information report . . .

GOVERNOR

He does it to economize, Laudisi. Having to maintain
two households . . .

SIRELLI

Well, we wouldn't criticize him from that viewpoint.
But really, Governor, do you believe a second wife
would take on the—

AGAZZI

[*Getting heated*]
The lowest household chores!—

SIRELLI

[*Continuing*]
For someone who was once her husband's mother-in-law and—to her—is a total stranger?

AGAZZI

Yes, yes, doesn't it seem a bit much?

GOVERNOR

It does, rather . . .

CENTURI

It certainly does . . .

LAUDISI

[*Interrupting*]
Too much for "a second wife"—if that's all she is.

GOVERNOR

[*Quickly*]
Let's admit—it *is* too much. Even this, however, can be explained—not, it's true, as generosity on her part —but definitely as jealousy on his. And, mad or not mad, he is jealous. That at least is established, it seems to me.

[*At this point the confused noise of many voices is heard from the music room.*]

AGAZZI

Heavens, what's going on in there?

Scene 7

THE SAME, AMALIA

AMALIA

[*Rushes in through the folding doors in the utmost consternation, announcing*]
Signora Frola! Signora Frola is here!

AGAZZI

No, by God! Who sent for her!

AMALIA

No one. She came of her own accord.

GOVERNOR

No, for heaven's sake! Not now!! Have her sent away, Signora!

AGAZZI

Yes, at once! Don't let her in! Stop her at all costs! If he found her here, he'd think it was an ambush!

Scene 8

THE SAME, SIGNORA FROLA, AND ALL THE OTHERS

Signora Frola enters trembling, weeping, imploring, a handkerchief in her hand, in the midst of an excited crowd.

SIGNORA FROLA

For pity's sake, good people, for pity's sake! You tell them, tell them all, Councillor!

AGAZZI

[*Coming forward, highly annoyed*]
I tell *you*, Signora, go away at once! You simply cannot stay here!

SIGNORA FROLA

[*Lost*]
But why? Why? [*To Amalia*] I turn to you, you are kind . . .

AMALIA

But look, look, the Governor is here—

SIGNORA FROLA

You, Governor. For pity's sake! I wanted to come to you.

GOVERNOR

Please don't be impatient, Signora. At the moment I cannot take care of you. You really must leave at once.

SIGNORA FROLA

Yes, I *am* leaving. I'm leaving today. I'm going away, Governor, going away for good!

AGAZZI

No, no, Signora. Please be kind enough to withdraw to your apartment next door for just one moment. Do me this favor. You can talk with the Governor afterwards.

SIGNORA FROLA

But why? What's the matter? What's the matter?

AGAZZI

[*Losing his patience*]
Your son-in-law is about to return. He will be here at
any moment. You understand?

SIGNORA FROLA

Will he? In that case, yes . . . I'll be going . . . I'll
be going at once. I only wanted to say this to you all:
for pity's sake, stop! You believe you're doing good
to me but you're doing me unspeakable harm! I shall
be compelled to leave if you keep on acting like this.
To be gone this very day and leave him in peace!
What in the world do you want of him—here—now?
What should he come here and do? Oh, Governor!

GOVERNOR

We want nothing of him, Signora, just don't worry. Be
calm and leave us, I beg you.

AMALIA

Please leave, Signora, please oblige us!

SIGNORA FROLA

Oh dear, Signora, you people are depriving me of the
only comfort I had left: to see my daughter, at least
from a distance. [*She starts crying.*]

GOVERNOR

Who says so? You have no need to go away. We are
asking you to leave the room for one moment. Don't
worry!

SIGNORA FROLA

But I'm thinking of *him*, Governor! I came here to intercede with you all for him, not for myself!

GOVERNOR

Very well. You needn't worry on his account either, I give you my word. Everything will be taken care of, just see.

SIGNORA FROLA

How? With all these people persecuting him?

GOVERNOR

No, Signora, that's not true. I am here, and I'm on his side. Don't worry!

SIGNORA FROLA

Thank you. You mean, you've understood . . . ?

GOVERNOR

Yes, Signora, yes. I have understood.

SIGNORA FROLA

We are satisfied to live in this way. My daughter is satisfied. So . . . Well, you attend to it . . . because if you don't, there's nothing for it but for me to go away. Just that: go away and never see her again, even from a distance as at present . . . I *beg* you to leave him in peace!

[*At this point there is a movement in the crowd. All start making signs. Some look back into the music room. Suppressed exclamations*]

VOICES

Oh dear . . . here she is, here she is!

SIGNORA FROLA

[*Noting the dismay and disorder, groans in per-
plexity and trembles*]
What's the matter? What's the matter?

Scene 9

THE SAME, SIGNORA PONZA, *then* PONZA

*The crowd divides up on either hand to let Signora
Ponza pass. She comes forward, erect, in mourning,
her face hidden under a thick veil, black, impenetrable.*

SIGNORA FROLA

[*Letting out a harrowing cry of frantic joy*]
Ah!!! Lina! Lina! Lina!
[*She rushes forward and embraces the veiled lady
with all the thirst of a mother who hasn't embraced her
daughter for years. At the same time Ponza is heard
shouting outside. Immediately afterwards he rushes
in.*]

PONZA

Julia! Julia! Julia!
[*Hearing his cries, Signora Ponza, though still in
the arms of Signora Frola, grows rigid. Ponza, coming
in, at once sees his mother-in-law thus desperately embracing his wife. He is furious and shrieks*]
Ah!!! Just as I said! Is this how you repay my good
faith? Cowards!

SIGNORA PONZA

[*Turning her veiled head, with almost austere solemnity*]
Don't be afraid, don't be afraid. Go!

PONZA

[*Quietly, lovingly, to Signora Frola*]
Yes, let's be going, let's be going.

SIGNORA FROLA

[*Who has withdrawn from the embrace, trembling all over, humble, echoes his words at once, urgent*]
Yes, let's be going, let's be going . . .
[*Ponza and Signora Frola embrace and exchange caresses. Their weeping makes a plaintive duet. Whispering affectionate words to each other, they withdraw. Silence. The company watches them until they have quite disappeared. Then everybody turns round, dismayed and moved, to look at the veiled lady.*]

SIGNORA PONZA

[*After having looked at them through her veil, says with dark solemnity*]
After this, what more can you want of me, ladies and gentlemen? There has been a misfortune here, as you see, which should remain hidden. Only in this way can the remedy work—the remedy our compassion has provided.

GOVERNOR

[*Moved*]
We should like to respect such compassion, Signora. We should wish you to tell us, however—

SIGNORA PONZA

[*With slow, staccato speech*]
What? The truth? It is simply this. I am Signora Fro-la's daughter—

ALL

[*With a gasp of pleasure*]
Ah!

SIGNORA PONZA

[*Without pausing, as above*]
And I am Signor Ponza's second wife—

ALL

[*Astonished, disappointed, in low voices*]
Oh! But . . . ?

SIGNORA PONZA

[*Without pausing, as above*]
And to myself I am no one. No one.

GOVERNOR

No, no, Signora, at least to yourself you must be either one or the other!

SIGNORA PONZA

No! To myself—I am the one that each of you thinks I am. [*She looks at them all through her veil just for an instant; and then withdraws. Silence*]

LAUDISI

That, my dear friends, was the voice of truth! [*He looks round at them with derisive defiance.*] Are you satisfied?
[*He bursts out laughing.*]

Appendix: The Source of Right You Are

"*Here is a dream: in it I saw a deep courtyard with no exit, and from that frightening image* Right You Are *was born.*" * *Between the dream and the play, however, came the short story, "Signora Frola and Signor Ponza, Her Son-in-Law."*

Though the adapting of a story to the stage needs neither explanation nor apology, it is perhaps proper to observe that in Italy the relationship between stories (novelle) and plays has always been especially close and that, of Pirandello's forty-four plays, only ten are completely independent of his stories, and twenty-eight might correctly be described as adaptations.

The adaptations were not always improvements, for while Pirandello regarded fiction as an elastic medium —a story could be any length, have any structure— in the dramatic realm he seemed to regard the three-act pattern as a Procrustes' bed. Even so successful a comedy as Right You Are *raises questions, and those who consider it* un*successful will doubtless prefer the story, their argument being as follows: "All that is essential in the play is in the story, which has something the play does not have, namely the device, beautifully handled, of a narrator who embodies the point of view of the town. The device by which Pirandello gets the townspeople into the play, on the other hand—namely, bringing them onstage one after the other—is a clumsy one. And to get a point of view into the play, he has to invent a character, Laudisi, whose limitation is that he is merely the author's point of view incarnate. Not only is the play overextended vertically (too many charac-*

* See *Almanacco Letterario Bompiani,* 1938.

*ters, too much talk in each act), it is overextended hori-
zontally—Acts Two and Three are redundant."*

*The fallacy in this argument is circular reasoning:
only what is in the story is essential, therefore everything that is added in the play is inessential. Which is
to overlook three points of principle. First, what was
not essential to the shorter work may* become *essential
to the longer; second, what is not essential to the story
form may be essential to the dramatic form; third, an
artistic element does not always have to be essential,
it only has to be advantageous. If preference of the
story is simply a preference of fiction to drama, there is
nothing more to be said; far be it from a drama critic
to pretend that an aisle seat in an auditorium is as cosy
as an armchair at a fireside. But, contrariwise, if you
are* in *an aisle seat, you will not bemoan the fact that a
play lasts two hours instead of fifteen minutes like the
story.*

*Though the expansion of a short story into a three-
act play is a hazardous enterprise, it may be called successful if the three acts—however inessential parts of
them may be to the original conception as we know it
from the story—justify themselves as drama. It is no
condemnation of* Right You Are *that it repeats things
that in the story are stated only once; the question is
whether, in their new context, the repetitions are effective or not. A question, possibly, which would never
have arisen had the play always been translated and
performed lightly enough. Once it has the rhythm of
farce, everyone would concede it the privileges of
farce, chief of which, as was stressed above, is manic
repetition.*

And Right You Are *is not merely longer than the*

*story, and more philosophical, it is also much larger
emotionally and spiritually. When Ponza and Frola
are no longer reported on by a third person but are allowed to speak for themselves, they acquire a stature
the story never approaches. To some extent, this is the
result of transference to the dramatic medium as such;
for the small characters of naturalism, to pass from
the pages of a storybook to the boards of a stage is a
sort of promotion. The "little man," who is such a
worm in modern fiction, is quite a bulldog in* Death of
a Salesman; *for in the theatre he has to speak for himself, and he has the actor to help him. This is not to say
that the change from narrative to drama has done Pirandello's work for him and that the actors will do the rest.
To changes that are automatic he adds others that require a genius for dramatic composition. In place of
the attractive solo which is the story he does the larger
job of orchestration which a play imposes: Laudisi,
the "crowd," and the Ponza-Frola trio have to be combined like woodwinds, brass, and strings. And if a
novelist's characters have something a playwright's do
not, and the latter's need the actors to fill them out, the
playwright's characters have something the novelist's
do not: they are not only characters but roles. Ponza
and Frola are interesting characters in both story and
play; in the play they are also great* parts.

*In noting the differences between the story "Signora
Frola" and the play* Right You Are, *it would be foolish to overlook the resemblances. I have so far spoken
as if the story, by contrast with the play, were of an
accepted sort, yet, in fact, it must seem just as eccentric
in the history of fiction as the play is in the history of
drama. An Italian critic has defined Pirandello's posi-*

tion in the evolution of narrative art in these words:

The novella *rests no longer on a fact but on a* trovata
(trouvaille, *brainstorm, conceit), no longer on a character-
study but on the presentation of a* maschera *(theatrical arche-
type). Hence the narrative is broken, convulsed, turbulent,
and the interest is not in the unfolding of the action, but in
separating out the moments on which the light has to be concentrated.**

*What interests the critic of fiction is that this kind of
story leads away from the main tradition of narrative.
What interests the drama critic is that it leads to the
theatre which is the proper place for concentrated light,
big moments, and turbulent action. The two greatest of
Pirandello's* trouvailles *are, first, the idea of characters coming onstage in search of their author and, second, the idea of a masker fixed in his masquerade for
life and building the eleventh century in the twentieth:
both ideas are theatrical in more than a figurative sense.
And what is a* trouvaille *after all but a coup de théâtre?*

* Giuseppe Petronio in his booklet *Pirandello novelliere e la crisi
del realismo* (Lucca, 1950).

Signora Frola and Signor Ponza, Her Son-in-Law *

YOU see that, don't you? It's enough to drive everyone right out of their minds, not to be able to figure which of them is mad, this Signora Frola or this Signor Ponza, her son-in-law. Such things happen only in Valdana. The unhappy town is a magnet for every sort of crackpot.

Either she's mad or he's mad, there's nothing else for it, one of the two *must* be mad. For it's a matter of nothing less than . . . but it's best if I begin at the beginning.

I'm terribly concerned, I can tell you, at the distress that has been the lot of every Valdanian for the past three months—it's not Signora Frola and Signor Ponza I'm worried about. It may be true that a great misfortune has befallen these two individuals, but it's also true that it's driven at least one of them mad and that he—or she—has been so helped out by the other that you just can't figure, as I said, which of the two it is that's mad. Now these people may know the best way of consoling each other, but what are they doing to our town? How *can* they? They make it impossible to judge —one way or the other. You can't tell fantasy from reality any more. It's agony, it's appalling, and it

---

* This translation is based on "La signora Frola e il signor Ponza, suo genero" in *Novelle per un anno*, 3d ed., Vol. II (Milan, Arnoldo Mondadori Editore, 1940). The writing of the story is conjecturally dated as 1917 by Pirandello's official bibliographer. The story has appeared in English as "A Mother-in-Law" in *The Medals and Other Stories* (New York, E. P. Dutton and Company, 1939) and as "Mrs. Frola and Her Son-in-Law, Mr. Ponza" in Luigi Pirandello, *Quattro novelle*, trans. by V. M. Jeffrey ("Harrap's Bilingual Series" [London, Harrap, 1939]).

doesn't stop: every day we see those two before us, look them in the face, know that one of them's mad, study and scrutinize them, examine them from head to foot—in vain! It's impossible to find out which is which! To find out where fantasy begins, where reality leaves off! And the dangerous notion naturally arises that it's six of one and half a dozen of the other—that any reality can quite well be a fantasy—or vice versa! Think of that!! If I were in the Governor's shoes, for the good of the people of Valdana I wouldn't hesitate to expel Signora Frola and Signor Ponza from our town!!!

But let's begin at the beginning.

This Signor Ponza came to Valdana three months ago as an executive secretary in the Government Building. He went to live in that new tenement on the edge of town—the one they call the Beehive. Over there. A tiny apartment on the top floor. It has three sad old windows on the other side, looking out over the country-side—the northern façade, facing all those pale orchards, has got in a sad way indeed, no one knows why, for it isn't old—and three windows on this side, in the courtyard ringed by the railing of a balcony divided into sections by an iron grill. On this railing, way up high, hang many baskets, all ready to be lowered at need on a rope.

At the same time, however, and to the astonishment of all, this Signor Ponza rented another small apartment, three rooms and kitchen, in the center of town— to be precise, Via dei Santi, Number 15. He said it was for his mother-in-law, Signora Frola. And in fact she arrived five or six days later. And Signor Ponza went to meet her at the station—went quite alone—took her to her new home and left her there alone.

Now of course we all understand it if a daughter gets married and leaves her mother's house to go and live with her husband—in another city if necessary. But if the mother can't bear being away from her daughter and leaves her house and her home town and follows her and then, in a city where she and her daughter are both strangers, goes and lives on her own— *that* we don't understand, unless we assume that husband and mother-in-law are so incompatible there can be no living together even in these circumstances.

Naturally, this is what everyone thought. And the loser in the general esteem was of course Signor Ponza. If anyone suggested that—in lack of sympathy perhaps, or sheer intolerance—Signora Frola must bear a small part of the blame, everyone else cited the maternal love that must be drawing her toward her daughter—and she not allowed to be with her.

It must be admitted that the appearance of the couple played a great part in arousing this general sympathy for Signora Frola and in creating the impression of Signor Ponza that suddenly took hold of everyone— namely, that he was a hard, and even a cruel, man. Thickset, neckless, swarthy as an African, with abundant and shaggy hair above a low forehead, thick, bristling eyebrows that join in the middle, the big sleek moustaches of a policeman, and in the dark, fixed eyes with almost no whites to them a violent and exasperated intensity that he only with difficulty controls, an intensity that could either be that of somber grief or that of contempt for others—Signor Ponza is certainly not the man to induce sympathy or confidence. Signora Frola, on the other hand, is a pale and delicate old lady of fine, indeed most noble, features. Her melancholy, though real, is not ponderous but sweet and airy. It doesn't stop her being very affable with everybody.

Now no sooner had Signora Frola given proof of the affability that was so natural in her than the general aversion to Signor Ponza increased; for the old lady's nature revealed itself to all as not only gentle, forgiving, tolerant, but also full of indulgent sympathy for the harm her son-in-law does her. And it was discovered that Signor Ponza not only kept the poor mother in a separate house, he carried his cruelty to the extent of forbidding her the very sight of her daughter.

"Not cruelty, not cruelty!" Signora Frola at once protests on her visits to the ladies of Valdana. And she extends her small hands, deeply disturbed that this can have been thought of her son-in-law. And she hastens to extol all his virtues, to say all the good about him that you could possibly imagine: what loving care he shows, how much consideration—not toward her daughter only but also toward her, yes, toward her, he is most attentive, selfless, oh, not cruel, no, for pity's sake! It's simply this: he wants his little wife all, all to himself, that's what Signor Ponza wants, he admits that she loves her mother, he gladly admits it, but he wants her love to come to the old lady indirectly, through him, *he* wants to bring it to her. Yes, it may look like cruelty, she sees that, but it isn't, it's something else, something that she, Signora Frola, understands perfectly but has difficulty putting into words. His nature, that's it—or rather, no, maybe it's a kind of illness, how can she put it? *Dio mio,* just look at his eyes, that'll settle it. Maybe they give a bad impression at first, those eyes, but to someone like herself who knows how to read them, they say everything, they tell of the fullness of the love in him, a closed world of love in which his wife is to live, she must never go out, and no one else come in, not even her mother. Jealousy? Yes, perhaps, if such a common word could sum up a love so total, so exclusive.

Selfishness? Yet a selfishness which gives itself utterly and provides a world to live in—for his own wife! After all, the selfishness would be her own if she tried to force her way into this closed world of love, to try and get in by force when her daughter is happy. Happy and adored. To a mother, that should be enough. For the rest, it's not true that she doesn't see her daughter. She sees her two or three times a day. She enters the courtyard of the house. She rings the bell and at once her daughter comes to the balcony above. "How are you, Tildina?" "Very well, Mother, what about you?" "As God wills, my daughter. Let the basket down!" And in the basket are always a few words by way of a letter with the day's news. That's all, and isn't it enough? That's how it's been for four years, and Signora Frola has got used to it. She's resigned to it, yes. It doesn't hurt her now.

It is easy to understand how this resignation of Signora Frola's, the way she says she got used to her own suffering, should—shall I say?—redound to the discredit of Signor Ponza, her son-in-law. And her working herself up into lengthy apologies only makes things worse.

It is therefore with real indignation—and I will also say with fear—that the ladies of Valdana, after Signora Frola's first visit, receive on the following day the announcement of another unexpected visit— from Signor Ponza, who begs them to see him for but two minutes if it isn't too inconvenient: he has a "declaration" to make which is "a matter of duty."

With burning cheeks, almost choking, his eyes

harder and more dismal than ever, in his hand a handkerchief whose whiteness, along with that of his shirt
cuffs and collar, is in appalling contrast with the dark-
ness of his complexion, hair, and suit, continually wip-
ing off the sweat that drips from his low forehead and
from the violet rash of his face, a sweat that proceeds
not from heat but from the obvious pressure of the violence he is doing himself (his long hands with their
long nails are trembling too), Signor Ponza confronts
the terrified eyes of the ladies in that same drawing
room and asks if his mother-in-law, Signora Frola,
paid them a visit on the previous day and if—here he
speaks with an effort, with ever growing agitation—if
she spoke of her daughter and if she said he absolutely
forbids her to see her and to go up to her apartment.

Seeing him so agitated, the ladies (as may easily be
believed) hasten to reply that, well, yes, Signora Frola
did speak of his forbidding her to see her daughter but
that she also said all the good about him that anyone
could possibly imagine, excusing him for that prohibition, clearing him of every trace of blame.

But instead of being quieted by the ladies' replies,
Signor Ponza gets more agitated than ever, his eyes
harder, more fixed, more dismal, the large drops of
sweat more frequent; and so, eventually, with a still
more violent effort to control himself, he comes to the
"declaration" which is a "matter of duty."

Which is simply this: Signora Frola, poor woman,
though she doesn't *seem* mad, *is* mad.

She's been mad for four years, yes. And her madness
consists precisely in believing that he doesn't wish to
have her see her daughter. What daughter? She is
dead. Her daughter died four years ago. And Signora
Frola went mad from grief at her death. Better so, for

madness was her escape from this grief. After all it was the only way she *could* escape it—to believe it isn't true her daughter is dead but that he, her son-in-law, refuses to let her see her.

In charity toward an unfortunate—as a duty, in fact—he, Signor Ponza, has been humoring her in her pitiful folly for four years, making many heavy sacrifices along the way: he maintains two households which cost him almost more than he can pay, one for himself, and one for her, and he obliges his second wife who, luckily, complies willingly in the spirit of charity, to help humor the old lady too. But there are limits even to charity, to duty, aren't there? If only in his capacity as a public official, Signor Ponza cannot allow the town to believe this cruel and improbable thing—that he would forbid a poor mother to see her own daughter— out of jealousy or anything else.

His declaration made, Signor Ponza bows to the astonished ladies and goes away. But before the ladies' astonishment has had time to subside a little, Signora Frola is here again with her sweet and airy melancholy asking to be excused if, because of her, the good ladies had suffered any shock at the visit of Signor Ponza, her son-in-law.

And Signora Frola, with the greatest simplicity and naturalness in the world, herself makes a declaration —but in confidence, for pity's sake! because Signor Ponza is a public official, and that's why he didn't speak out the first time, don't you see? Because his career might be seriously affected. Signor Ponza, poor man— as secretary in the Government Building above reproach, efficient, correct in all his actions, in all his thoughts, a man simply full of good qualities—Signor Ponza, poor man, is—on this one point—not reasonable. Poor man, it's *he* that's mad. And his madness consists precisely in this: he believes that his wife died four years ago and goes about saying that *she,* Signora Frola, is the mad one because she thinks her daughter still alive. No, he doesn't say this to justify his almost maniacal jealousy and the prohibition against seeing her daughter, no, poor man, he believes, seriously believes, that his wife is dead and that this present wife is his second. A sad story indeed! Loving his delicate little wife all too much, this man had come near destroying her, killing her—they had had to take her away from him in secret and shut her up in a sanitarium without his knowledge. Well, the unhappy fellow, whose head had already been turned badly enough by that frenzy of love, went quite mad. He believed that his wife was really dead. And the idea fixed itself in his head till he couldn't get rid of it, even when, about a year later, his wife, in the best of health again, was brought back to him. He believed it was someone else. His friends and relations had to get together and go through the pretense of a second wedding. This completely restored his mental equilibrium.

By this time Signora Frola believes she has reason to suspect that her son-in-law has been entirely sane for a while and is pretending, only pretending to believe this wife is his second, so he can keep her all to himself, out of contact with everybody, for perhaps, in spite of everything, the fear flashes across his mind that his wife could be taken from him in secret again.

Yes. Or how could you explain the way he takes care of her, the mother-in-law, all the attention he gives her —if he really believes he now has a second wife? He wouldn't feel himself under such an obligation toward one who actually wasn't his mother-in-law any longer

—now would he? Signora Frola says this, mind you, not as further evidence that he is the mad one but to prove to herself that her suspicion is well founded.

"Meanwhile," she concludes with a sigh that takes the form, on her lips, of a sweet and most mournful smile, "meanwhile the poor girl must pretend she is not herself but someone else. And I must pretend I am mad and believe my daughter still alive. It isn't very hard, thank God, because she is there, my daughter is healthy and full of life, I see her, I talk to her, but I am condemned not to live with her, I must see her and talk with her from a distance, so that he can believe, or pretend to believe, that my daughter, God forbid, is dead and that this wife is his second. But I say again, what does it matter if in this way we succeed in bringing peace to both of them? I know my daughter is adored and happy, I see her, I speak to her, and for love of her —and him—I'm resigned to living like this and being thought mad. We must be patient, Signora. . . ."

Now: don't you have the impression that we all have our mouths agape and our eyes popping out of our heads? That the whole town of Valdana is out of its senses? Which of the two to believe? Which of them is mad? Where does reality leave off? And fantasy begin?

Signor Ponza's wife could tell. But she is not to be trusted if she says she's his second wife—in front of him. Nor is she to be trusted if she says she's Signora Frola's daughter—in front of her. One would have to take her to one side and have her speak the truth confidentially. Impossible. Mad or not mad, Signor Ponza really *is* jealous and won't let anyone see his wife. He keeps her up there under lock and key as in a prison, and the fact undoubtedly favors Signora Frola, but

Signor Ponza says he is forced to act this way, and in fact that his wife insists on it, for fear that Signora Frola should unexpectedly drop in on her. It could be a pretext. There is also the fact that Signor Ponza doesn't even keep a maid. He says this is just to economize—he has to pay the rent on two households. And he himself does the daily shopping. And the wife who, according to him, is not the daughter of Signora Frola, in compassion for the poor old creature who was once her husband's mother-in-law, does all the housework, even the lowest drudgery, without recourse to a maid. It seems a bit much. But it's also true that this state of affairs can be explained, if not as compassion on her part, as jealousy on his.

Meanwhile Signor Ponza's declaration has satisfied the governor of the province. But Ponza's appearance is not in his favor, nor is a great deal of his conduct— in the eyes of the ladies of Valdana, who are all more inclined to believe Signora Frola. The latter has been most anxious to show them the affectionate messages her daughter has let down in the basket and many other private documents. Signor Ponza destroys their value as evidence, however, by saying that they have all been written just to bolster the pitiful deception.

At any rate, this much is certain: that the two of them show, the one for the other, a marvellous spirit of self-sacrifice that is most touching; each shows for the (assumed) madness of the other the most exquisitely compassionate consideration. Each of them argues with the sweetest reasonableness; in fact no one at Valdana would ever have dreamed of saying either of them was mad if they hadn't said it themselves— Signor Ponza of Signora Frola, Signora Frola of Signor Ponza.

Often Signora Frola goes to see her son-in-law in the Government Building to ask his advice about something. Or she awaits him at the end of the day to go and buy something with him. For his part, every evening and very often in a free hour during the day, Signor Ponza goes to see Signora Frola in her furnished apartment. Whenever they meet on the street by accident, they proceed together with the utmost friendliness. He politely walks at her left, and, if she is tired, offers her his arm. And they walk on together—amid the anger or amazement or distress of the people who study and scrutinize them, examine them from head to foot—in vain! They are still totally unable to comprehend which of the two is mad, where fantasy begins, where reality leaves off.

Notes

PRELIMINARY. The world première of this play took place at the Teatro Olimpia in Milan on June 18, 1917. By 1924 it had reached Dullin's Atelier in Paris; by 1925 the Lyric, Hammersmith, London; by 1927, the Theatre Guild, New York. In the French, English, and American productions, respectively, the part of Laudisi was played by Charles Dullin, Nigel Playfair, and Reginald Mason; that of Ponza by Corney, Claude Rains, and Edward G. Robinson; that of Signora Frola by Marcelle Dullin, Nancy Price, and Beryl Mercer.

The play was first published in the periodical *La nuova antologia* in 1918. The present English version is based on the definitive text in the collected works, viz., *Maschere nude*, Vol. II (Milan, Arnoldo Mondadori Editore, 1948). The Italian text has also been published in America, though with one short piece of bowdlerization, by D. C. Heath and Company in 1930, with introduction, notes, and vocabulary by Joseph Louis Russo; the only English version previously published is that of Arthur Livingston * in *Three Plays* by Luigi Pirandello (E. P. Dutton and Company, 1922), reprinted with some slight changes in Luigi Pirandello, *Naked Masks: Five Plays*, edited by Eric Bentley (Everyman's Library [E. P. Dutton and Company, 1952]).

The new stage version was commissioned by Roger L. Stevens for performance at the Brattle Theatre, Cambridge, Massachusetts, in 1952 under the direction of the present editor. It was used, again under his direction, at the Westport Country Playhouse in Connecticut in the same year. In these two productions the part of Laudisi was played, respectively, by Philip Bourneuf and Alfred Drake; that of Ponza by Martin Gabel and Martin Kosleck; that of Signora Frola on both occasions by Mildred Dunnock. The play has also been televised in this version by Kraft Television.

The present editor first provided suggestions for a production of the play in *The Rocky Mountain Review* (Winter, 1946), in an essay entitled "Pirandello and Modern Comedy" which was subsequently incorporated in his book *The Playwright as Thinker*. His introduction to *Naked Masks*, re-

* (1883–1944), Professor of Italian at Columbia University.

printed in the book *In Search of Theater,* also includes a
passage on *Right You Are.* For further literature about the
play, the reader is referred to the general Pirandello bibliog-
raphy in Appendix III of *Naked Masks.* To this might be
added the article "Una tragedia italiana," by Giorgio Pros-
peri, in the magazine *Sipario,* November-December, 1946.
The editor has read many reviews of English and American
performances; has cited W. J. Turner's (below, page 163),
which appeared in *The New Statesman and Nation,* October
3, 1925; but would wish to cite only one more, Stark Young's,
which originally appeared in *The New Republic,* March 23,
1927, and is now more easily accessible in Mr. Young's vol-
ume *Immortal Shadows.*

RIGHT YOU ARE. This title has been used simply because so
many people know the play by it. Also because no one has
ever found an apt translation of the Italian *Così è (se vi
pare).* The first American edition is called *Right You Are (If
You Think So!).* At the first English performance, the title
was *And That's the Truth!* Ludwig Lewisohn suggested *As
You Like It,* and Arthur Livingston *And Thinking Makes It
So.* Other attempts are *Right You Are (If You Think You
Are)* and *Have It Your Own Way.* Literally, the Italian means
"Thus it is if it seems thus to you," but this is impossible
English; the nearest one can come to it is *It Is So (If You
Think So),* a title imposed upon the Livingston translation
by the present editor in the Everyman's Library Pirandello.
What no English version has rendered is the comical con-
trast between the pontifical main clause *(Così è)* and the
colloquial parenthesis *(se vi pare).*

CHARACTERS. "The administration of an Italian province
is entrusted to a *prefetto,* appointed by the premier, assisted
by a varying number of *consiglieri*" (Russo). *Prefetto* is here
translated as governor, as the word *prefect* is not, in this
meaning, in the Anglo-American vocabulary; *consigliere* is
left as councillor, this being less misleading than any other
word. The Italian for executive secretary reads simply *segre-
tario,* but it is essential to understand that he would have
workers under him and is not merely a clerk.

THE PLACE. THE TIME. In the short story which is the source of the play (see Appendix) the town is called Valdana, a made-up name. But we are told on page 21 where Ponza and Frola come from, namely, a village in Marsica. Marsica is "a district in the Abruzzi bordering on Lazio. It was ravaged by one of the most terrific earthquakes of modern times on January 13, 1915. Avezzano, the most important town in the district, lost about 90 percent of its population of 11,500, Pescina had 4,500 victims, while some of the villages in the vicinity were literally wiped out. The total loss of life amounted to more than 30,000" (Russo). It is these facts * that give plausibility to the Ponza-Frola family's total loss of identification papers.

Page 3. ACT ONE, SCENE ONE. The scene divisions of the Italian edition have been kept. In general (though Pirandello is not absolutely consistent), a new scene starts with the entrance or exit of an actor or actors. These scene divisions are very useful in rehearsing the play, especially since a list of the characters appearing in each scene is given at the head of it.

THE CURTAIN RISES. In Italy it is quite usual to wait half an hour for latecomers, after which the playwright can plunge in medias res, as Pirandello does here, and as we in England and America, who start pretty much on time, simply dare not do. The opening scene in the Anglo-American theatre has the function of keeping the punctual part of the audience happy while the unpunctual part gets seated. Now the punctual people are the earnest and analytic people, the people likely to think that, in *Right You Are,* the social and historical background should be clearer. For their sake, in the Brattle Theatre production, a series of slides was projected on a curtain, which thereby became a screen. Lester Polakov had been to the New York Public Library and had found actual photographs of the 1915 earthquake. The pictures were preceded, accompanied, or followed by headlines, making a sequence as follows:

* Which deeply influenced another Italian writer: Ignazio Silone. See *The God That Failed,* ed. Crossman, pp. 92 ff.

Slide One: JANUARY 15, 1910—REGION OF MARSICA RAVAGED
  BY EARTHQUAKE
Slide Two: photo with legend: AVEZZANO BEFORE
Slide Three: photo with legend: AVEZZANO AFTER
Slide Four: 11,500 DEAD IN AVEZZANO ALONE
Slide Five: photo of more ruins
Slide Six: FIRST SERVANT OF OUR STRICKEN PEOPLE HAS BEEN
  OUR KING
Slide Seven: photo of Victor Emmanuel III inspecting ruins
Slide Eight: THE FAMILY, THE FAMILY, FOREVER THE FAMILY!
  —VICTOR EMMANUEL III
Slide Nine: photo of Victor Emmanuel in the bosom of his
  family
Slide Ten: HIS SUFFERING PEOPLE—SURVIVORS OF THE EARTH-
  QUAKE
Slide Eleven: photo of survivors amid ruins
Slide Twelve: photo of survivors living in tents
Slide Thirteen: MARCH 5, 1910—GOVERNOR OF OUR PROVINCE
  DECORATED BY KING FOR MASTERLY HANDLING OF DISPLACED
  PERSONS
Slide Fourteen: photo of Governor (i.e., of the actor cast for
  the role)
Slide Fifteen: IN OUR TOWN, COUNCILLOR AGAZZI PROVIDES
  GOVERNMENT JOBS FOR HOMELESS
Slide Sixteen: photo of Councillor Agazzi (also an actor)
Slide Seventeen: MAY 10, 1910. COUNCILLOR AGAZZI DECO-
  RATED BY GOVERNOR FOR SAVING SITUATION
Slide Eighteen: photo of Agazzi being decorated
Slide Nineteen: IN OUR TOWN THERE ARE NO DISPLACED PER-
  SONS, THERE ARE ONLY BROTHERS AND SISTERS—AGAZZI

The date was shifted from 1915 to 1910 because our Anglo-
American audience associates the former date too readily
with the First World War and knows nothing of the earthquake anyway. It would be desirable to show the Governor
being decorated by Victor Emmanuel in the above sequence
if photographers could solve the problem of getting the his-
toric king together on one picture with a member of the
current cast. Some directors might like to use such slides
before Acts Two and Three, in which case the following sequence is suggested.

Act Two:

Slide One: JULY 3, 1910—POLICE COMMISSIONER CENTURI TAKES UP PONZA CASE

Slide Two: photo of Centuri in uniform

Slide Three: WHEN IN DOUBT ASK A POLICEMAN—TWENTIETH-CENTURY PROVERB

Slide Four: JULY 4, 1910—CENTURI OPENS UP ARCHIVES. STAFF OF FIFTY TO STUDY RECORDS OF ALL BIRTHS, DEATHS, AND MARRIAGES

Slide Five: THE SPIRIT KILLETH BUT THE LETTER GIVETH LIFE —CENTURI

Act Three:

Slide One: JULY 25, 1910—CENTURI TO ANNOUNCE FINDINGS TODAY

Slide Two: COUNCILLOR AGAZZI TO APPEAL TO GOVERNOR IF NOT SATISFIED

Slide Three: photo of Governor in Mussolini-like pose

Slide Four: THE GOVERNOR IS ALWAYS RIGHT—OLD ITALIAN SAYING

Page 28. LET'S SET THE STAGE. MOVE YOUR CHAIRS BACK A LITTLE. And later the chairs are moved in again in several stages as the gossips get more and more interested in their visitors' narratives. These two lines are interpolations necessitated by the stage business. "Let's set the stage," it is true, is not absolutely necessary. It is a gag suggested by the nature of the particular action, the character speaking, and the whole play: the "chorus" is always setting the stage for the drama of the Ponza-Frolas. "Let's set the stage," a line never used by Pirandello, is repeated a number of times in this version and, in production, culminated in a big laugh on the very last repetition (the Governor's use of it in Act Three).

Page 57. ACT TWO, SCENE ONE. Pirandello situated the second and third acts in the study adjoining the drawing room of the first act. Where a revolving stage is available, the easiest solution is to place both rooms on it, with each room almost as wide as the proscenium arch; so that in Act One, we can see just a little of the study, and in the following acts, we can see a little of the drawing room. But what to do if

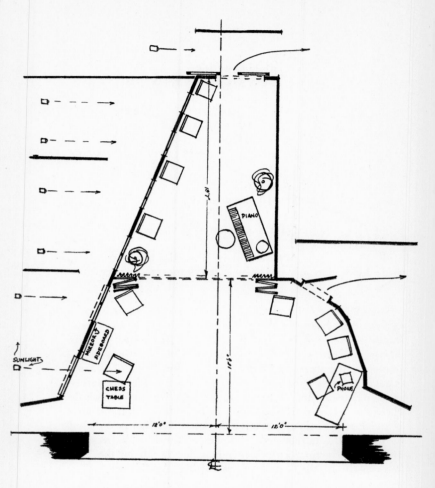

Ground plan of the Brattle Theatre production, 1952. Lester Polakov, designer

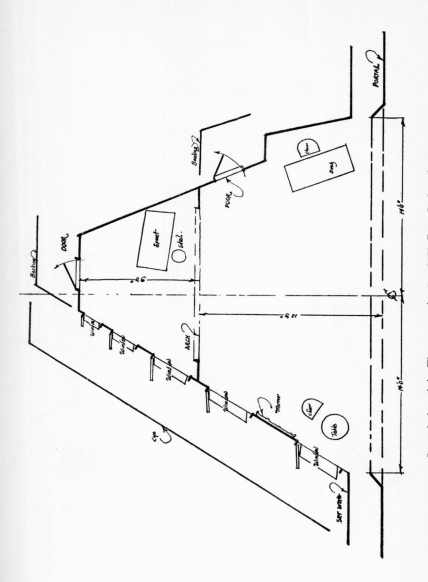

Ground plan of the Westport production, 1952. Peter Larkin, designer

there is no revolving stage? Pirandello himself envisaged two sets with a complete change of scene between the first two acts. Then, in the second act, when he wants to introduce sounds from the drawing room, he has them spoken in the wings—and "wings" is the word, as it is clear that he thinks throughout in terms of the baroque tradition with entrances left, right, and center.

Against following the playwright's lead there are two arguments of quite different kinds. The first is purely practical and perhaps purely American: the cost of building two sets is too high. The second is that "voices off" from the wings now seem very old-fashioned or simply ineffective. (Signora Frola plays the piano in one room, Signor Ponza overhears her from the next. Would it not be better if we could see *both* parties?) It was with these two arguments in mind that I asked Lester Polakov to devise a scheme whereby the two rooms could be presented to the audience simultaneously. His ground plan is shown on page 154; the effect from out front is indicated by the drawing on page 27. In the Polakov arrangement, the main action all takes place in the drawing room, but there is another room behind it (upstage), called the music room because the piano is in it, yet also functioning as a corridor or entrance hall to the drawing room by virtue of its oblong shape. It is in fact one of the two entrances to this set; the butler brings Ponza and Frola through it in Act One. The other entrance, leading directly to the drawing room, is used whenever there is no time for the more ceremonious and, as it were, processional entrance. The music room can be completely open to the drawing room, as it should be in Act One. It can be curtained off—as for the music scene in Act Two. Or it can be shut off by folding doors —to shut out the crowd in Act Three. In the handling of this crowd, incidentally, the dual set has many advantages, most notably, that dialogue can be audibly spoken in the drawing room while a rather noisy crowd is on stage but in the music room. In Act Two, the sudden unveiling of Frola at the piano is much more theatrical than her entrance from the wings could be. And there is one respect in which the dual arrangement assists the drama throughout. If the drawing room is rather garish and in bad taste, the music room can be macabre and dark. Such a contrast is to be found in many an Italian palazzo, where you arrive at the plush, modern living room through ancient and unlit galleries. Polakov's drawing room was a bureaucrat's showpiece (over the folding doors was Victor Emmanuel in stained glass; on the walls, trophies from Tripoli; chairs in gilt and gold on the floor; and above the doorway the motto *Veritas*), while the music room, at the bidding of the lighting man, could veer from Robert Adam to Charles Addams, and seemed to bring in Ponza, Frola, and, above all, the Veiled Lady from another world.

In Acts Two and Three, the stage directions, and very occasionally the dialogue, have had to be adapted to this staging. Producers who wish to revert to the original arrangement should have little difficulty in doing the necessary rewriting for themselves. In any event, the earlier English version, which follows Pirandello in this respect, is at their disposal.

Page 66. THE LARGE MIRROR. Lester Polakov had the ingenuity so to set the angle of the mirror that a good portion of the audience could see Laudisi in it: the little vaudeville act is greatly improved if what we see is only an image while what we hear comes from a face we cannot see. The speech itself proved the hardest bit in the play to English. As far as the sense goes, the trouble mainly stems from our not having a word for *fantasma*. The homonym *phantasm*, in spoken dialogue, means precisely nothing. The Italian word being both abstract, like *fantasy*, and concrete, like *ghost*, the former word has been used earlier in Act Two where an abstraction was called for, the latter in Act Three, where the joke is that the crowd thinks Laudisi refers to an actual spirit. The mirror speech is the bridge between these two passages, and for that reason both words, *fantasy* and *ghost*, have been worked in. Such an exigency forces the translator, of course, into a heavier style than the original. Even so, the solution is not complete. Pirandello talks of carrying your *fantasma* inside you, and a *ghost* has never been considered so portable. There is also a problem in communicating Pirandello's brand of relativism in *any* English words, since Anglo-Saxon readers tend to assume he is saying that everything is unreal and truth is nowhere to be found, whereas what he is trying to say is that everything is real and truth is everywhere to be found. The mirror itself arouses expectations Pirandello does not gratify. What we are prepared to get is the simple contrast (as in E. E. Cummings's *him*) between the *me* I know and that part of *me* which other people know. Pirandello is out for bigger game!

Here are three alternative versions of the speech, beginning with the most literal one. The second, the clearest and most explanatory version, is the worst as English speech and therefore as theatre; and here is the problem in a nutshell: we have to carry over Pirandello's meaning, yet it is even more urgent to give the actor something (literally and figuratively) to play with.

1. Ah, so there you are! Well, old fellow, which of us two is the madman? Yes, I know, I say *you* and you point at *me*. Come now, between you and me, we understand each other pretty well, the two of us. The only trouble is, the others don't see you as I do! So what becomes of you, my dear chap? The "you" that is seen by other people—what must it be for me? Why, a creature of fantasy, a figment, an idea, an image. Well, you see *these* madmen? They ignore the image they carry in themselves—in their own souls—and, driven by curiosity, go running after images of other people—thinking those are quite a different matter.

2. Ah, so there you are! Well, old boy, which of us two is the madman? Oh yes, I know, I say *you* and you point your finger at *me*. So far, so good: between the two of us, well, we understand each other, don't we? The only trouble is, the others don't see you the same way I do. They simply have an idea, a conception, of you. That is, you only exist in their imagination, you're a figment, a creature of fantasy. Now what can *I* make of their idea of *you*? Well, I can have an *idea* of it—and so you become, for me, an idea of an idea, a conception of a conception. So—even for me—you're a figment, a creature of fantasy—a ghost. Every man jack of us carries such a ghost in his breast. But do we act accordingly? By no means. Most of us prefer to ignore what we carry within ourselves—our idea of other people's idea of ourselves—and to go running after something more external—our idea of other people, which we believe to be no idea at all, no ghost,

no fantasy, but sheer reality, sheer truth. This is what our friends here are doing, driven by the demon of curiosity.

3. (Laudisi is shaking his own hand and echoing Sirelli) Goodbye, Lamberto, goodbye, Lamberto! Lamberto? Who's that? Where is he? Where? (Seeing his image in the mirror and drawing a long breath) Ahh! So there you are! Signor Lamberto, good morning! And, by the way, old boy, which of us two is the madman? Yes, I know, I say *you* and you point your finger at *me*. But I know you pretty well, don't I? Or do I? I know you at pretty close quarters anyway. I know you a little better than I know the others. You're not me of course, I don't know me, you're—an image in the glass. But *other* people! They're an image in a less reliable glass than this, a much less literal-minded glass. I see other people only in the distorting mirror of my own mind. In fact what I take for other people—why, they're just creatures of my own fantasy, phantoms, ghosts, and what other people take for me, *that's* not me, it's *you*, Signor Lamberto. And, what's more, it's you as they see you and not you as I see you! You know *these* madmen? "Let's set the stage, Signor Ponza will be sitting here, I'll put Signora Frola there . . ." They don't waste much time looking at their *own* image, do they? They concentrate on hunting down other people. And they don't realize they're only hunting their own fantasies, the Ponza *they* take him for, the Frola they take *her* for . . .

Page 69. SIGNORA NENNI. It is hard to understand why Pirandello left Signora Nenni silent for so long. On the assumption that she is a great listener, it is possible to have her silently repeating with her lips what Laudisi says. Certain key words that have been on her mind might even become audible, in which case Laudisi will have to hear her and respond. For example, *Laudisi:* A forged document, understand? *Signora Nenni* (grasping at the fascinating and appalling word): Forged?! *Laudisi:* Forged. And then again a few seconds later, *Laudisi:* Signor Ponza comes along and says they're forged. *Signora Nenni* (indignant this time, as at the discovery of treason): Forged! *Laudisi* (mimicking her horror): Forged. No longer embarrassed at Signora Nenni's being left out of the scene, the director will now have to take care she doesn't monopolize it; the device amuses the audience so much that the actress playing Signora Nenni will repeat every word Laudisi utters unless she is forcibly restrained from doing so.

Page 79. WITH THAT MAN. Some audiences are more quick-witted than others. A director who decides that his audience is slow-witted should assume that they have not, at this point, grasped what Agazzi's "great idea" is and that it must be restated. A restatement can be interpolated here in Dina's speech by deleting "with the man. If he found them closed . . ." and substituting the following: "with Signor Ponza. The doors must be left open so we can be heard talking in the music room. Father will use this as an excuse to bring us all in here. With Signora Frola. If he found the doors closed and couldn't hear a sound from the music room . . . Well, you know Father." At the end of Laudisi's next speech, after "convinced," the following can be added: "already that it's Ponza who's mad?"

Page 8. NINA MAD THROUGH LOVE. Pirandello names this 18th-century opera (by Paisiello) but does not give a name to the melody he describes. The only tune in the opera which the description seems to fit is a soprano aria, "Il mio ben, quando verrà?" And what makes one fairly certain that this is what Pirandello referred to is that the aria has appeared in modern song collections, whereas a score of the opera is practically impossible to come by. The American producer will find the item in *Italian Songs of the Seventeenth and Eighteenth Centuries,* published by Schirmer. Only an actress who can play the piano fairly well will be able to manage the performance herself, for the piece, being a song and not a piano solo, is printed in three clefs. It also entails technical difficulties such a playing three against two.

Page 90. BURSTS OUT LAUGHING. Since Act Two would send the audience into the lobby in much the same frame of mind as Act One, it might be shrewder to have no intermission at all at this point. If the stagehands need a couple of minutes to rearrange the furniture, the music from the preceding scene can be played again. It could even be sung this time by a soprano appearing before the curtain except that the modern audience is far too well educated and will ask what such a little entr'acte "symbolizes."

Page 91. ACT THREE, SCENE TWO. It is not worth presenting a crowd unless it can be both large and well trained: ideally, we should see a cross section of an Italian town from the postman to the priest, from the schoolmaster with his books to the farmer's daughter carrying chickens home in a basket. Since at Westport the crowd that was provided two days before the opening looked like *La Traviata* at a girls' college, it was eliminated altogether; it may be useful to prospective producers to know that the play works quite well without a crowd—or rather that the cast without extras can itself seem quite a crowd. With or without extras, this scene is the most dangerous one of the play in that there is a strong chance of its dragging, and the moment is the one above all others— half an hour before the end—when a play must not drag. The problem is to give Laudisi's intellectual fooling all the physicality of farce. This can be done by building the earlier part of the scene as a chase, a rushing from one side of the stage to the other and back again in pursuit of the elusive harlequin. In the later part of the scene (beginning with "Columbus's egg"), Laudisi is no longer pursued; he is the pursuer. He can force the "crowd" into a clump and buzz annoyingly around them like a wasp. He can even resume his teasing of Signora Nenni whenever he comes near her. She will naturally be fascinated by the word "ghost" and the repetition-gag can be brought to an hysterico-farcical climax with the phrase "to doubt it" if Laudisi refuses to let her have the last word and repeats her repetitions in a mad to-and-fro until the others clasp their heads and scream. The first turning point ("Columbus's egg") where Laudisi puts in Sirelli's head the idea of bringing Signora Ponza over is followed by a second ("you're all sure she exists") where Laudisi plants the notion that she is a ghost. At each turning point the action must, as it were, shift into a higher gear, so that top speed is reached at the announcement of the Governor's arrival.

Page 98. THE GOVERNOR'S OPINION. *Right You Are* is the story of a contest between Ponza and Frola, a contest for *credence,* and everyone in the theatre is betting on the issue. First, Signora Frola is the favorite, then Ponza comes out in front, then Frola leads again, and so forth. Pirandello is at pains to keep the race a close one: whoever had the last word has always got ahead but has always been followed by a last word from the other. Yet, although the two have been evenly balanced in actual power, there has been no balance in the sympathy that has been aroused: it has all gone to Frola. And a danger in any production of the play is that the audience's sympathy for Frola may place them conclusively on her side. It is to deal with this danger that Pirandello brings the Governor in. He is Ponza's only real supporter, but being Governor his authority is assumed (in the Italian context) fully to counterbalance that of all the Agazzis and hoi polloi combined. In a way, it is but the pattern of the second act all over again. Frola gains steadily in sympathy, but her position is then assailed by sheer *force majeur.* Ponza's change of mood is so abrupt we *have* to believe him: how could he have calmed down so quickly if the outburst had not been deliberate? In the third act, against Frola's charm and sincerity are marshalled the authority and worldly wisdom of a governor. By the time Signora Ponza makes her concluding announcement, the betting out front should be even. Whether it is so or not will depend principally on the actor playing the Governor. The part needs a Sydney Greenstreet.

Page 99. COLUMBUS'S EGG. When once the way has been shown, nothing is easier than to follow it. Columbus applied this principle to his voyages by asking on a famous occasion if any present could make an egg stand on its end. When the others had tried in vain, he struck the egg gently on one end, then stood it on the broken part. Producers of *Right You Are* who think their audience will not understand Laudisi's exclamation can change it to "Eureka!" (though perhaps it is better to risk mystifying half the audience if there is some assurance that the other half gets the point; the mystification, in any event, is slight; and few people, when they are mystified, know it).

Page 103. THE GHOST OF A SECOND WIFE IF SIGNORA FROLA IS RIGHT. THE GHOST OF HER DAUGHTER IF SIGNOR PONZA IS RIGHT. Actors will ask, "Shouldn't it be the other way round? After all, it's Ponza who believes it's a second wife and Frola who thinks it's her daughter." Exactly: if Ponza is right, Frola's daughter is not there, Frola only imagines this, creates the fantasy or ghost of it, and vice versa. But by this time you could probably say the opposite and few spectators would know the difference.

Page 114. SUBVERSIVE ACTIVITIES. If the phrase seems not to belong to 1910 it can be dropped. Literally, the Italian means "the headquarters of a conspiracy" (the word "conspiracy" is also still to be seen in our newspapers). In any case, the actor should not try for a laugh on the line or it will kill what often proved the biggest laugh in the play, which comes immediately afterwards on "Let's set the stage."

Page 115. FEROCIOUS INVESTIGATION. This passage, it may be noted in passing, is translated literally.

Page 128. THICK VEIL, BLACK, IMPENETRABLE. In the American première of 1927 Armina Marshall's veil was not impenetrable or even thick, and two years earlier, on the occasion of the London première, the poet and critic W. J. Turner had suggested that Signora Ponza should wear no veil at all. It is true that, on the literal plane, nothing would be given away by her not wearing a veil. Seeing the lady's face, we still receive no shock of recognition; we do not know her. But, it might be retorted, that is why the revelation can only be an anticlimax—aside from its being contrary to Pirandello's instructions and, more important, to the meaning of his play—on which latter point, see page x.

Page 129. DON'T BE AFRAID. How should the lines of Signora Ponza be spoken? The formal, almost hieratic, style of the lines encourages the actress to attempt some formalized style of utterance. The present editor can only say that in his experience the role has been more effective when played as a real woman with natural emotions. The tone of her first

line can be firm, helpful, loving: the only kind of formaliza-
tion the line needs is, perhaps, that the first "don't be afraid"
be spoken to Ponza, the second to Frola, the "Go!" to both.
The tone of the lines Signora Ponza speaks to the crowd
should be ironic, gently bitter. She despairs of having them
really understand, so she (deliberately?) provokes them with
a riddle; and whether she knows it or not, there is one present who will understand: Laudisi, whose laugh will grow
out of the silence following his very quiet "Are you satisfied?" and carry the meaning of the riddle to that outer
world, the audience. After "I am Signora Frola's daughter,"
there is a long intake of breath from the crowd; at last the
secret seems to be out. A little more deliberately, perhaps
mockingly, Signora Ponza adds: "And I am Signor Ponza's
second wife." General and utter confusion. Then her tone
sinks to a lost sadness for: "And to myself I am no one. No
one." By this time even the imperturbable Governor is per-
turbed. "No, no, Signora," he stammers, "at least to yourself
you must be either one or the other!" There is exasperation
in his "must be" as if to say: "you really can't upset a governor's equanimity this way, how unreasonable can life get?"
Signora Ponza delivers her parting shot with an absolute
calm and simplicity, "Sono colei che mi si crede," which
means "I am that one who I am believed to be." Like the title
of the play, this key line defies pithy, idiomatic translation.
"I am whoever you choose to have me" is wrong in two re-
spects. *Colei* does not mean "whoever" but "that particular
woman," a difference with broad philosophical implications.
Nor can the impersonal *si crede* be translated "you choose"
in this context, for the "you" will seem to refer to the governor, who has just spoken. In both his productions, the
present translator used the line "I am she who each of you
thinks I am," the "each of you" justifying itself by reference
to Pirandello's philosophy: the veiled lady is not merely she
who the governor thinks she is, or she who people collectively
think she is, but she who each man separately and differently
thinks she is. Yet the phrase "she who," though it can be put
over in the theatre by a pause between the two words, seems
rather queer, and actresses are tempted to say "she who*m*"
which makes matters worse. So for this book another version

has been hazarded: "I am the one that each of you thinks I am." Even this demands a slight pause (after "the one").

Page 130. BURSTS OUT LAUGHING. One of the nicest problems of the performance is: what to do with Laudisi's laughs at the end of each act? The editor's memory of a great production at the Comédie Française in 1938 is that, each time, the whole stage was dimmed out except for a spot on Laudisi's face and that the laugh which came from the pinpoint of light * was quiet, sardonic, regular—an even, Mephistophelean ripple. At Westport, this lighting and this type of laughter were used only at the end of the play. In the other acts it was thought best not to cut Laudisi off from the others—he had been off in his corner quite enough—but to play up his relationship to them. In the first act, Alfred Drake changed "You're looking each other over?" to "You're looking for something?" and then, as they blankly returned his amused gaze, was overcome by a great gust of good-humored laughter. In the second act, the couch, upon which the action of the whole had been centered, was exploited by Laudisi. He stood behind it and feigned surprise at not finding Ponza and Frola seated there. Ringing laughter was again used, but this time harshly, sarcastically.

* And from the throat of Jean Debucourt.